BUSINESS CHAMELEON

BUSINESS CHAMELEON

A Practical Guide to Success for Managers

LÁSZLÓ KÁROLYI

KÁROLYI
BUSINESS SOLUTIONS

BUSINESS CHAMELEON
A PRACTICAL GUIDE TO SUCCESS FOR MANAGERS

iUniverse books may be ordered through booksellers or by contacting:

iUniverse
1663 Liberty Drive
Bloomington, IN 47403
www.iuniverse.com
1-800-Authors (1-800-288-4677)

ISBN: 978-1-4917-5341-5 (sc)
ISBN: 978-1-4917-5342-2 (e)

Library of Congress Control Number: 2014921667

Printed in the United States of America.

iUniverse rev. date: 12/23/2014

CONTENTS

FOREWORD

We gladly accepted László Károlyi's invitation to introduce his book, which will undoubtedly be profitable reading for anyone taking on a managerial position. We are sure we can draw inspiration from this series of practical examples forming the chapters of a management story and so many real-life situations—some successful, others less so—offering tips and suggestions of some kind.

Management is a difficult art that allows, over time, across the seasons of the year and of each of our lives, teams to move forward toward improvement and success, while giving each and every member the possibility of growing and maturing.

In these few words of introduction, we would simply like to highlight a handful of parameters that we consider important to remember in the management of people. First, though, we need perhaps to get back to basics for a moment, just to remind ourselves of what it is we call *management*.

While the English term *management* has been adopted by the French Academy, which recommends a French pronunciation—we are unsure of the rule in Hungarian—it is interesting to note that the words "manager" and "management" are actually derived from the French words *ménager* and *ménagement*, which according to the Collins Robert French Dictionary mean "handling with care."

A manager is someone capable of using the means available to achieve the best possible results. László Károlyi focuses on the management of human resources, and this is clearly where a true manager's real added value lies. We would like briefly to highlight just a few key ingredients of these considerations on management:

- It seems to us that to manage a team effectively, you need to acknowledge a variety of personalities and often cultures and therefore to encourage both individual and group expression to foster both diversity and tolerance—in other words, to facilitate coexistence. This has become all the more essential now that travel is so much easier today that people, especially within Europe, can very easily move from one country to another in pursuit of work. Facilitating coexistence therefore also means mixing new recruits and experienced staff on the same teams, where each will be able to contribute specific added value.

- We might add that a team needs optimism, objectives, and vision, though it is not always easy to provide such a perspective. A good manager will focus efforts on specific objectives, inspiring trust and confidence in others by setting them challenges that can be met successfully. This way, the loop of success becomes a virtuous circle that generates progress.

- Effective management requires an ability to provide meaning and give bearings by clearly situating each decision in time and in its context, by "telling the story" that led to these decisions, relying on the intrinsic need for meaning, transmission, and cultural enrichment.

- Effective management requires relating one's action to the outside world, to society, to the economic and sometimes political background, and trying to anticipate potential developments. Though by no means always easy, thinking ahead to the future can be a key to supporting one's decisions.

- Effective management requires listening and being attentive to what your team is saying—and also to what they may not be saying, being able to decode silence and the unspoken word.

- Last but not least, we should like to stress the need for managers to be recognized for their ethical and exemplary behavior. You cannot expect others to do what you do not demand of yourself. Consistency in what you say and do is essential. This is called *congruity*.

There is of course a lot more to say on this topic, but we shall leave that to the author of this valuable book. The above is merely a glance at some of the aspects we wished to highlight, which you will find addressed in more detail in the pages that follow.

Enjoy your read.
Gilles Schnepp
Chairman and Chief Executive Officer of Legrand Group
Edith Dumas
Former Legrand Group Vice President, Internal Communications and External Relations

PREFACE

All life battles teach us something, even those we lose.
—Paulo Coelho

You must learn from your battles if you want to reach your goals. In my opinion, in today's dynamically changing world, it's more important than ever to expand our knowledge base and promote good decision-making by acquainting ourselves with the experiences of others and by analyzing and evaluating them. This book presents the reader with thought-provoking stories and experiences collected at the frontier between theory and practice, between the global and local, with advice drawn primarily from business life. Given that it focuses on people, teams, and efficient cooperation, I think that it may help readers make good decisions not only in the business sector but also in other areas of life. According to an old proverb, a wise man learns from someone else's mistakes. Turning that into the positive, I would say let's learn also from one another's successes.

Many management gurus have described their own approaches as to what to do and how to do it in order to make an enterprise prosper. In the global world, at times of crisis, one must often venture into new hunting grounds or find a new way around a familiar hunting area that's changed. Any idea may be useful at such times, and what's more, it is almost risk-free to draw on the experience and ideas of others. Experience obtainable that way is obviously badly needed while facing protracted economic uncertainty and a foggy, uncertain business environment. Reliable planning is limited to the short term, and one is often forced to make decisions based on partial information, but nevertheless, there are and there will always be good ideas to help develop companies.

In recent years, I have often seen assessments from analysts sounding the death knell for the future because of the difficulties of the economic environment. These difficulties notwithstanding, I think Franklin D. Roosevelt had a point when he observed that "there are as many opinions as there are experts." In many respects, economic developments resemble the changing of the seasons, with inconvenient and more popular periods alternating. We're all entitled to our opinions, but we have to make decisions and develop activities in all seasonal conditions.

Transition is slow sometimes, as if time had come to a standstill on a sweltering summer day or a humid late autumn day wetted by soft rain. At other times, however, a gust of stormy wind suddenly turns everything upside down. That is how it is in the economic environment too. Farmers may note sadly the damage caused by an unexpected storm; nevertheless, they start anew each year. Of course, they learn the lesson and try whatever they can to protect the crop with new solutions against changing environmental effects. And if such guarantees take into consideration the environmental impact and do not exploit nature, the cycle can be assessed as one that represents a development system sustainable in the long run.

Sustainable, efficient, and effective operation under changing conditions: that is the ideal goal. That is the task of company management in the most basic terms. What you need for this is knowledge, experience, and someone to produce results—that is, a human being, the manager.

Knowledge can be acquired, but experience is a matter of time and opportunity. With time, our deposit is finite; there is nothing we can do about that. As for opportunity, the problem is the component of risk that goes with it. You can learn from a failing project or business plan, though naturally in such cases one would much rather collect the lessons as an external observer than the person responsible for the task.

That is why I thought it might be useful to many if I shared some of my managerial experiences of the past thirty years. The business environment in which I had to perform and the companies in which this happened changed like the seasons. There were sunny days, but there were also tougher, harder times. The experience kept accumulating, in local and global enterprises in Hungary as well as in other countries worldwide. Efficient and effective operation and making the most of opportunities—that's how you might summarize the expectations for a leader. What is needed for that, however, is neither machinery nor money but good managerial decisions and a good team. In other words, the key to results and efficiency is man himself.

To make decisions, you need information—not only the process metrics but also methods, analyses, and opinions. Sometimes good ideas strike while you're reading a novel or watching a movie. This is the arsenal of the manager, from which he chooses according to the situation. The theoretical arsenal, on the other hand, is complemented by experience.

—László Károlyi

INTRODUCTION

This book amalgamates theory and practice into short, thought-provoking stories. In principle, you can start reading the book at any point, and you can put it down whenever you like. One story takes only a few minutes, so you can finish it no matter what important and urgent tasks await you according to your planner. And if, under the impact of reading the stories or because of some oddity of life, an idea worth noting down occurs to you, jot it on the *pro memoria* pages. This way, the book will become an ever-expanding storehouse of useful experiences.

How successful a manager or team leader will be depends strongly on how wide is his know-how and how wise and creative he is in their use. This book's stories provide useful links between theory and practice, between global and local, and serve as a compass to guide you to the right decision. The real value creation comes from a good team and visionary managers, those who can identify business opportunities in a fast-changing environment and find creative solutions—not just cut-and-paste—in multicultural environments.

To be more successful, you need a solution-driven approach. Creativity and innovation open hidden gates for often very simple business and management solutions. Like nature, business is a continuously changing and cyclic environment. To find the right answers and reach the right solutions requires different approaches depending on the situation. To be successful, you need to adapt your practice like the chameleon adapts its color.

Sixty stories are divided into four sections using the metaphor of seasons. Fifteen stories for each season give you a handhold for good times and bad. There are stories for autumn, when the world is changing; for winter, when new solutions should be sought out instead of the old ones to start the engine of the economy anew; for spring, when you struggle with the difficulties of implementing new conceptions; and for summer, to harvest the results and strike a healthy balance between work and private life. The fifteenth and final story in each chapter is written by a guest writer and presents an issue related to the chapter but from a different point of view.

Change is part of business life. Let's accept it and look for solutions—there are always some who manage to find them. I hope that this pilgrimage between ideas, situations, and sometime feelings will help the reader find new and creative ideas that highlight the hot topics and give inspiration to find the right solution for sustainable business development.

Charles Darwin said, "It is not the strongest of the species that survives, nor the most intelligent, but the one most adaptable to change." The aim of *Business Chameleon* is to give a practical guide to business success and to develop management and even nonmanagement problem-solving acumen and inspiration. To be successful in business and in life, we need to develop the chameleon capacity to adapt our colors depending on the changing environment. We should accept that the environment is always changing. Those will survive who can best manage change.

CHAPTER 1

Autumn: Changing Environment

1.1 THE THREE Cs

We are all faced with a series of great opportunities—
brilliantly disguised as insoluble problems.
—John W. Gardner

The three Cs represent a triad that managers should never lose sight of: change, customers, and competition. In the dynamic three-C interplay, there are rhapsodic, fast-changing economic *circumstances*; offer-dominated markets where the *customer* is king; and *competition*, with its global and local actors, representing the stage where we need to recognize the winning moves.

Change is present everywhere. Of course, sometimes we don't even realize that time is passing. After the graduation ceremony, for example, the secondary-school friendships last for a little while before the globalized world gets you. People disperse, and when they meet again in ten years' time, they marvel at how much the others have changed. But *everything* keeps changing and developing around us—technology included. Where has the time of Commodore desktop computers and of the large mobiles gone? They have been forgotten, although we are speaking of no more than a few decades. We welcome many novelties and are averse to others, but that does not change the fact that everything is changing, whether you like it or not. In the world of business, you must adjust to the changes or you will be ousted from the market, losing your customers and maybe even your business.

Hardly twenty years ago, I requested a landline phone; at that time, there were no other options, and that's how it was done. I was hoping that the line would be installed within just a few months because the confirmation had the serial number 4 on it. Some months passed and nothing happened. I thought I'd inquire as to the status of my request, hoping to be able to accelerate the process. The response to my polite question as to when I could expect to have the line installed was "I don't know."

"How come?" I asked. "I'm fourth in line. Why is it impossible to know the date?"

This sounds like a joke today, but in the early 1980s, this was reality in former socialist countries or maybe even in rural areas of the United States. True, I was fourth in line, but the local telephone exchange center could not be expanded any further. "The line will be connected within a few months after the new exchange is ready," a voice assured me. But no one knew when the new phone exchange would be ready. No one would have thought then that the development of mobile technology would sweep away the monopoly of the providers of landlines. No competition existed yet in that field.

Change may be slow, as in the case of the emergence of mobile-phone services, giving ample ground for traditional service providers to alter their business strategy. Change, however, can also be much faster, as in the case of the global financial crisis of 2008. Some—such as investors and general contractors of resort villages on the Spanish coast, for example—could not switch fast enough, since they did not have sufficient time to adjust.

Adjustment, however, is a must, since a business requires customers. Customers, in turn, must be won over and retained. If customers' expectations change, business managers must find the appropriate answers unless they want to put their enterprise on a negative course.

There is an abundant choice of business literature offering various solutions and methods, but these often relate to examples that do not apply fully to the east central European environment. However, I have read one book that is worth reading by all who work in sales. This is Harvey Mackay's *Swim with the Sharks Without Being Eaten Alive: Outsell, Outmanage, Outmotivate, and Outnegotiate Your Competition.* Most pieces of advice there are useful and worthy of consideration. The following quotation from the introductory chapter provides an excellent summary of who makes a good salesman: "The winner is never the one who grasps a major order. *The professional is always recognizable by the fact that the customer returns to him.*"

Perhaps this is the best advice you might give someone working in sales or managing a sales team. Other useful lessons follow in Mackay's book. The first one, entitled "It's Not How Much It's Worth, It's How Much People Think It's Worth," tries to guide the reader into understanding the basis on which to define what you have on offer. A good salesperson is where a business opportunity presents itself. He understands what the customer needs and gives an offer that can function as the basis of a long-term business relationship—an offer that is good for the customer.

The real challenge, however, is competition, the last of the three Cs. Globalization, the free flow of goods and services, the information revolution, social restructuring, and the spread of individualism have each played a role in the growth of competition. Competition may be good for the consumer in the short term, yet it forces businesses to wage cutthroat development and price wars.

Competition is unavoidable. Nevertheless, every well-managed enterprise strives to attain a monopoly position, if only temporarily, through professional know-how or individual solutions to issues in goods or services, or simply via marketing. This is an excellent strategy for business development. While in a monopoly position, one can gather strength for the next round of cutthroat price competition.

Change has been, is, and always will be a part of our lives, but it is not the whole picture. The business world is inconceivable without customers. Competition is something we would be willing to give up

3

for a while, but it's unavoidable. These are the three Cs that determine the contemporary market environment of the twenty-first century. They represent both an opportunity and a threat.

Don't just look. See, and you will find the opportunities.

1.2   DANGER OR OPPORTUNITY?

The brave man is not he who does not feel afraid,
but he who conquers that fear.
—Mark Twain

I have heard from many that an economic crisis cripples and destroys companies, workplaces, lives. I do not dispute that a crisis is a hard and stormy period that may cause serious damage, but it may also help a lot in remedying difficulties—if we view an economic crisis as, for example, the rainy season. In the autumn, we know that rain will come, and it may last for weeks without even a breath of wind, but it may also come suddenly, with strong winds and thunder and lightning. Some changes are quiet and long-lasting, while others are stormy and swift.

Weather today causes increasingly inconvenient, extreme surprises; in the same way, one will have to prepare for extreme business situations. But don't forget that this is nothing but change—albeit faster, more unexpected, and hence more dangerous change. Life is continuous change. You may be afraid of it, but you must not be alarmed at it. You must adjust. If the flood comes, build higher. If lasting cold is expected, store fuel. All this is a learning process. It is not always convenient, but it is necessary for survival.

In crises, under pressure, we may make some bad decisions, but we also make good ones. Making adjustments and looking for solutions are indispensable for the latter. One of my favorite citations comes from Darwin's book *The Origin of Species*: "It is not the strongest of the species that survives, nor the most intelligent, but the one most adaptable to change." This has become known as the law of evolution, but one could not gain a better perspective when it comes to the successful management of a business than that provided by hundreds of thousands of years of evolution. This is why it is important to treat difficult situations not as crises but as changes of some kind.

Size up the situation realistically; look for trends and solutions rather than for reasons why something cannot be done. If you don't, someone else will certainly find the right answers. It is generally true that the problem is not what life has brought about but the way you react to it. It is instructive that, in Chinese, the words for *danger* and *opportunity* are amalgamated into one ideogram. The character containing the two signs side by side means "change." The message is that by adopting that approach to the difficulties in your life, you have a chance to overcome them.

Crisis is change, just as when the seasons change. It may be fast or slow, but it is always cyclical. If the change is fast and harsh, a rapid response is needed. By insisting on ways of operating that proved successful in better times, even if you can see that they may not work under the changed conditions, you may bankrupt your business. If you think there is no solution, the same thing might happen. However, if you are able to prepare for extreme times, to change and bring about change matching the circumstances, you will find new opportunities. Do not focus on why you have landed in a given situation and what you cannot do, but rather on how to proceed.

Never deem a situation hopeless; there is always a solution. Do not give up trying—find it!

1.3 GOALS REMAIN EVEN IN THE ASHES

The tragedy in life doesn't lie in not reaching your goal. ...
It isn't a calamity to die with dreams unfulfilled,
but it is a calamity not to dream.
—*Benjamin Elijah Mays*

Here is a story I read in *A 3ʳᵈ Serving of Chicken Soup for the Soul*:

Thomas Edison's laboratory was virtually destroyed by fire in December, 1914. Although the damage exceeded $2 million, the buildings were only insured for $238,000 because they were made of concrete and thought to be fireproof. Much of Edison's life's work went up in spectacular flames that December night.

At the height of the fire, Edison's 24-year-old son, Charles, frantically searched for his father among the smoke and debris. He finally found him, calmly watching the scene, his face glowing in the reflection, his white hair blowing in the wind.

"My heart ached for him," said Charles. "He was 67—no longer a young man—and everything was going up in flames. When he saw me, he shouted, 'Charles, where's your mother?' When I told him I didn't know, he said, 'Find her. Bring her here. She will never see anything like this as long as she lives.'"

The next morning, Edison looked at the ruins and said, "There is great value in disaster. All our mistakes are burned up. Thank God we can start anew."

Three weeks after the fire, Edison managed to deliver his first phonograph.

This story demonstrates to me that there are accidental events, sometimes even painful and apparently inconvenient, that nonetheless transform occurrences into opportunities for those who have set objectives—but only for these types. Aimlessness means your life is driven by the principle of "whatever will be, will be." Then it turns out, sooner or later, that this way, nothing will be. Edison's example shows that it is never too late to set yourself objectives. Of course, if you start sooner, you are more likely to attain some of those objectives.

Consider the story of Steven, who has been working for Big Ltd. for five years. He started his career at a small private company and came over to us after four years. He was a good professional, he got the hang of the job rapidly, and what was even more important, he brought new ideas. Those who consider production a routine chore are wrong. Part of it is, but you can and must innovate everywhere. Those who drop behind in this will lag behind the competition and wake up one fine day to see they have no customers left. Of course, only one battle of the war for the customer is waged in production, but that's where added value is created. New ideas as well as perseverance and managers responding to change by finding new solutions to issues are a must.

Well, Steven was like that. By the end of the third year, he had become deputy plant manager. He made it to the group of employees with high potential, participated in training, and introduced many new ways of operating and doing things. His performance was generally acknowledged. Finally, after the plant manager retired, the long-expected moment came for Steven to take his place. Five years of work had brought him the recognition he was looking for—he had attained his goal! Of course, as usual, after the first three days of happiness, one sets new goals to be reached. Steven was no exception.

At the same time, the company management set the ambitious target of introducing new, more competitive methods into the production process—a combination of Lean and Kaizen, the American and Japanese ways of treating various production activities and processes in a new way. The essence is production driven by customers' needs, with the optimization of activities deemed valuable by the customer and the elimination/minimization of processes considered to be neutral—such as inventory, since the customer pays for the product, not for the storage. The "just in time" technique, one component of the Lean method, states that, ideally, you should manufacture what the customer orders when he orders it, and no more. The principle is simple, but the more complex the product portfolio, the more difficult it is to realize it.

Quality is a value recognized by the customer, and this is what the philosophy of total quality management (TQM) puts in the foreground. Administration, on the other hand, has no value, so it is to be retained only to the minimum extent necessary for management;

yet it should show visually, in a way that can be easily understood by managers and subordinates alike, the efficiency of the system's operations. It is important that all should know whether targets have been met or there is a backlog.

The list of principles redrawing the production process components could be continued (takt time, 5S, TPM), but the crucial thing here is that none are customary methods in east central Europe. So there was a legion of tasks—operating and project work—and the introduction of new methods. Steven rose to the challenge, as usual, and achieved good results in one year, including several introductions. The relevant pilot systems performed well. At the year-end performance assessment, as in previous years, he got a maximum rating. However, he declared that he wanted to develop and learn and was eager to face new challenges.

This was an unexpected request. We were in the middle of the process of implementing Lean, so there would be ample opportunity to learn and face challenges at the company for many years to come. A series of consultations began between the HR manager and Steven. Finally, the issue was put before the managing director. He tried to find a solution and discussed his proposal with the headquarters of the group. He considered Steven a valuable person, so he requested a permit for Steven's employment abroad for six months at a subsidiary after the end of the Lean project. Local experiences can be profitable anywhere, and Steven would find the new environment useful and motivating. The proposal for Steven to go on a mission abroad was approved, but he chose not to take it. He thought that his experience and professional knowledge should get him farther. At the next discussion, he admitted that a few years earlier he had set himself the goal of becoming production manager within five years.

That time has passed, and Steven has finally attained his goal—albeit at another company, for a few months after this discussion he left Big Ltd. A company in a distant corner of the country was looking for a production manager, and Steven filled the vacancy. As Sándor Csoóri said, "To believe in something is not the solution, only the beginning of the solution." Steven believed in his goal and did everything to attain it. Had it been otherwise, he would not have found the opportunity and then grasped it.

This story, however, has yet another message. Whether you are a manager or an employee, you must not forget the principles and values of the company and the team you are working with. Choose for yourself a place where you feel all right, as you will be spending one third of your life there. But have your own individual values as well. If you change jobs, besides the financial considerations, values must be among the criteria.

Without aims, you will drift. Decide what you want and act on it.

1.4 REPLACING THE COPYING METHOD

He that will not apply new remedies must expect new evils;
for time is the greatest innovator.
—*Francis Bacon*

The year 2002 was a most exciting one for the South Korean national football team, the Tigers. South Korea and Japan hosted the seventeenth FIFA World Cup together that year. This was the first such event held in Asia. Brazil and Germany made it to the finals, and Brazil won the tournament 2 to 0. The most interesting point, however, is that the Tigers were the first Asian team to make it to the semifinals, and they ended up fourth. This was indeed a great result considering that the team, composed of members showing outstanding individual performance, had never made it to the World Championships before; their trajectory had always come to a dead end in the group rounds. In 2002, the coach of the team was the Dutch Guus Hiddink, and given these antecedents, his work cannot have been at all simple.

Why? Imagine a social culture based, traditionally, on respect, to the point where it is relevant to how you express your thanks. If the person is older, you must say "kamsahamnida," and if he is younger, you need to use another word conveying less respect: "gomaw." The team play of the Tigers had also been influenced by paying tribute. In the case of passes, the player did not necessarily pass the ball to someone in a good position to shoot at the goal but to an older and hence more authoritative person. This may have contributed to the peace of mind of the team's players on the football field, but it was definitely not beneficial in a world championship, where the older, more authoritative person may have had no chance at all of getting into a better position.

Guus Hiddink solved the issue of mandatory expression of respect by introducing a joint meditation session in the changing room where the players could apologize to one another in advance for playing on the field driven by the logic of football and not with regard to traditions. At the end of the match, they had another meditation session in the changing room, where the younger ones apologized and the older ones excused them for disobeying the social rules. The results spoke for themselves. Apart from the fourth-place finish mentioned above, the South Korean national football team has won the Asia Cup twice.

What is the message of this story for businesspeople? Do not try to copy techniques that were tested and effective in other places, as this may lead to failure. This is what would have happened had Guus Hiddink, encouraged by his previous successes, tried to use his usual techniques on the field. Instead, the coach tried to detect and understand what was causing a problem. It was probably not easy for him, being of Dutch nationality, to find out how to keep a tradition of thousands of years away from the football field! But since instead of copying he looked for a solution in a creative way, he managed to make the Tigers leave their social habits in the changing room and focus on effectiveness and winning. A manager has to do the same within a company: look for solutions in a creative way to solve problems and handle situations encountered, which will bring success to the company even at the cost of overwriting the habits and beliefs of employees (if this is necessary).

Alexander's company introduced a computerized system developed for MRP2 (manufacturing resources planning). The comprehensive company and production management system is a tool whereby the company management can gain access to fast and up-to-date information. The product of the US-based QAD company has been introduced with success in eighty countries the world over, and more than 3,200 businesses now use it. The objective is to make decision-making more effective, optimize costs, and reduce inventories while enhancing customer-service efficiency.

Based on the principle that "whatever comes from the United States must be good," Alexander's project team took on the well-defined processes, rules, and organizational arrangements without feeling a need for any changes. They copied everything without any examination and analysis of local conditions or processes. The system went live and seemed to be all right, producing the expected results. People mastered their respective tasks. The managers calmed down, and the project was closed. "This is the routine operational phase, and everything is all right, the installation was a success," Alexander said.

Six months later, however, one of the indicators—measuring the performance of a partial process—started to slant. It was more and more often below target value. Then another followed suit. Within a few weeks, the key indicator portraying customer service also fell below the targeted level.

"No problem," the team said at the monthly evaluation meeting. "This is a professional system. We'll locate the processing point responsible for the poor results based on partial indicators. We'll twist the regulators a little." The idea was that if they merely adjusted the parameters, everything would be all right. And that is what they did—yet in two months' time, customer service faltered, and they were in trouble. This time, the performance of another area began to go out of alignment and then returned to normal, though a month later the customer-service indicator deteriorated again.

Alexander suspected that there was something wrong, and not without reason. A year passed before it was realized that twisting the parameters of the high-end system would be in vain; the problem had to be different, as performance was showing only a slight improvement, and the investment wasn't producing any returns either.

Soon, an emergency unit was set up under Alexander's leadership. The members spoke to people, analyzed procedures, reviewed plans and the installation memoranda, and thought a lot, looking for causes. They came to the conclusion that culture, operations, and—in general—the frame of mind of Eastern Europeans is somewhat different from those of people in the United States. Although we live in a global world, there are similarities between all persons, and given parameters may even be identical to ones in a system designed for American conditions, local specifics ought to have been taken into consideration in the process design. The copying method had failed.

This produced quite a headache and a delay of almost one year in achieving the expected results. Two corrections had to be made, one regarding organization and the other a process regulatory alteration to give the system an Eastern European flavor. An excellent performance in the last eight years has confirmed the findings of the team led by Alexander: think globally, but never forget local properties and endowments.

First understand how it works, and adopt only what applies.

1.5 CHANGE YOUR POINT OF VIEW

The reasonable man adapts himself to the world; the unreasonable
one persists in trying to adapt the world to himself.
—*George Bernard Shaw*

There was a plan that my wife and I would go with a group a friends to the Kazan Strait for a long weekend at Whitsun. The strait is delimited by the Romanian Almás mountains, a part of the Carpathians, to the north, and by the Serbian Miroc to the south. The landscape was beautiful, covered with uninterrupted green vegetation in the spring. The Danube is narrowest there, at a mere 150 meters. The cliff towers above the water at a height of 300 meters, and a winding road follows the demarcation line between the mountains and the Danube. This view is worth riding a motorcycle for, which was the plan. We would have started together, the ten of us, on five motorbikes, but for some reason the two of us lagged behind the others that day.

We traveled leisurely, at our own speed, admiring the landscape, and we fled from a rain shower at a wayside inn for the afternoon. We therefore arrived late, but joined the group; yet it was worth it even for this single night. The atmosphere was excellent, and we had great conversations. The next day, we started back home to Hungary together. We forgot about the leisurely speed and rode without looking around, at high speed, negotiating the flows of water across the road and tricky points in a road covered in gravel or mud. I had to concentrate, and I was always being forced to make quick decisions, such as brake or accelerate. This was the situation for almost a hundred kilometers. Of course, I had to pay attention to the others as well.

Along the way, it came to my mind that this was like the everyday decision-making procedure at the company I was a manager of. Watch the performance of the team and take risks, to a healthy extent. If the road is straight, you are bound to become inattentive sooner or later. You proceed at your usual pace, and there is nothing to shift you from your comfort zone. In times of crisis, however, you need to concentrate with all your senses to survive. But change is everlasting, like the weather. At times everything is motionless, at times all suddenly becomes dramatic, as with a sudden rainstorm during a time of good weather in the summer. If general economic circumstances become more difficult, competition will be keener. A rival may cause some surprises, even in more peaceful times, and you may abruptly be torn from your leisurely speed and end up in a crisis zone.

How, and on what basis, should a manager decide where the limits of healthy risk-taking lie? If this were a simple issue, there would be no accidents on the road and no bankruptcies in business life. Before making a decision—a good one, of course—you have to weigh the odds. Weigh what is to be gained if a decision leads to success and what may be lost if it is conducive to failure. If the impending loss might be excessive, proceed with caution.

I like to take risks, but only if I have a chance of assessing their feasibility, of seeing the possibilities as well. Of course, sometimes there is no other choice but to rely on your intuition. Nevertheless, I think that the feeling and experience of risk are useful—if possible, not in a crisis or on a slippery road, but rather during nice weather. I am aware of the maximum capacity of the technology at my disposal; I know how strong the team is and how strong I am and what the road conditions are, and I take risks accordingly. It is equally true that I would not push my luck in times of crisis, just as I would not put the motorbike into top gear on the most difficult terrain. If something happens in nice weather, there will be time to stop and repair things, but at a time of crisis there will be too little or no time for this. In such cases, you may get along with solutions you have tested already. Just as it is a good idea to practice driving or riding a motorbike on a training ground and experiment with special situations under safe conditions, in business it is commendable to practice, prepare, and make plans under optimum conditions. You'd better have a second, backup scenario ready at all times.

Someone who is alone, traveling the road like a lone wolf, may move at his own pace. In a group, however, even if he is the leader, he must take account of the dynamics of the group and the opinions of others and people's capacities to move forward. If not, he will be an outsider, irrespective of the number of his companions. Sooner or later, he will be rattling alone, and results will also stop.

> **It doesn't matter whether you drive in a group or alone—your goals will not change.**

1.6 "CRENCHMARKING"

If you are afraid to make mistakes, you will never be successful, for you will have no opportunity to learn. You will have no way to find out what works and what doesn't. Mistakes are messengers. They inform you that you do not know the circumstances or the factors at play well enough yet. Every mistake is also an opportunity to change direction.
—Richard Marcinko

A good idea is always useful, particularly in times of trouble. And if you already have an idea, it is worth making it work. What is a good leader like and what makes a good team, one that knows what to prepare for both before and after the storm and is capable of finding good solutions in any situation?

Many surveys and analyses have been made to try to find the elixir of the successful company and management. One of the best known is probably Jim Collins's book *Good to Great*, in which he investigates 1,500 companies in an attempt to find the common properties of the most successful. Collins chose companies whose value increase had exceeded the growth of the stock-exchange index by at least three times for a period of at least fifteen years over the past forty. He found eleven such companies altogether. According to the analysis, they had the following traits in common:

- managers who were modest leaders, with strong professional wills
- target-oriented organization with consistent implementation, and with the right person in the right place
- realistic status evaluations
- an output-oriented, disciplined corporate culture
- innovations
- reliance on the convincing effect of results

At a professional forum, the head of a Hungarian company investigated the listed companies in a similar way, but from a completely different angle. He took companies with a business policy that had incorporated the philosophy of sustainable development and demonstrated compliance by regular reports, and compared their performance to that of the average stock-market index of the past twenty years. Unfortunately, the sad result of the survey was that companies assuming a pioneering role in disseminating the principle of sustainable development tended to underperform in terms of share performance.

But let's take a look at yet another analysis. This one puts the employee under the microscope. Marcus Buckingham and Curt Coffman of the Gallup Organization surveyed 80,000 managers and 1 million employees over twenty-five years. The goal was to get an answer to the question, "What makes a workplace good and effective, what makes the employee loyal to the workplace, and what encourages them to perform well?" The results were first published in their book *First, Break All the Rules*. The empirical answer is provided by the respondents to the following twelve questions addressed to employees:

1. Do I know what they expect of me at my workplace?
2. Is access to materials and equipment needed for the job ensured?
3. Are work tasks and job organization based on personal skills and competencies?
4. Do I get regular weekly feedback as well as praise?
5. Does my superior care about his subordinates as human beings?
6. Am I encouraged to develop?
7. Does the opinion of the employee count?
8. Is the work I do important for the goals of the company?
9. Is everyone committed to quality work?
10. Do I have good friends at the workplace?
11. In the past six months, has my progress and performance been discussed with me?
12. Have I had the opportunity to learn new things in the last year?

These are useful points, ones worthy of consideration, though the Gallup survey is but one of many. The Harris Poll adopted a somewhat different approach. In its survey, 23,000 people from the United States—persons who worked full-time and in senior jobs in sectors deemed important—had questions put to them. The results were surprising. For example, only 37 percent of respondents were aware of the goals of their organization, while only 15 percent felt that the company provided the necessary conditions by which they could attain their aims.

We could well keep on listing surveys and evaluations, looking at what makes a company more effective and efficient. Once we know what makes the best companies good, all that remains is to learn and copy their methods, so that we, too, will be better. However, if everyone copies the same models, sooner or later there will be no substantial difference between companies—or will there?

This "karaoke capitalism" trap is highlighted by a book of the same name by John Ridderstale and Kjell A. Nordström. In the authors' opinion, karaoke reality is a cosmopolitan club where we are flooded with countless options that, in reality, are nothing but institutionalized imitations. By giving preference to best practices, management theory and practice have transformed the world of business into a karaoke super-factory. The final outcome is sameness, something "uniformly perfected" that is unfortunately not feasible in a situation of free economic competition. The economic ideal will thus never be reached: the more similar the products or services of two companies, the more decisive will be the role of people from the point of view of performance. As competition intensifies, performance will deteriorate because of management and operational errors. Thus, new ways of doing things will need to be found, and processes must be improved. The engine of the competition is the creative idea and the human being who realizes it: the leader and his team.

Various analyses have shown that it is actually possible to work efficiently and effectively in the long run. Benchmarks and best practices are needed for this. (Sometimes it is not bad to also study worst practices—i.e., examples of failure.) Yet those who do nothing but imitate cannot excel; they cannot make a competitive edge out of this.

Companies creating new ways of operating by putting ideas and experiences they have gathered through a creative grinder do acquire a temporary competitive edge—a monopoly, so to speak. They manage to get the consumer's attention by showing customers blinded by supply dumping a new color. Such a flash may be sufficient to lure them over. For this to work, though, a good team is needed, and of course a good leader, someone who can get some business advantage out of creative benchmarking ("crenchmarking"). It is not worth spending energy on things that have been invented already. Draw on such items, certainly, but don't make copies. Add your own ideas, a pinch of creativity, and success is bound to come.

To make crenchmarking work, you need a masterly harmony of only three things:

- a creative, new, better solution to an issue based on benchmarking and best practices
- a list of advantages of this new or better way of operating or product
- involvement of employees in successful implementation

Crenchmarking is not a cure-all for every situation, but the really good companies have always been capable of mobilizing employees to attain their targets and of promoting an innovative atmosphere. And what is this if not crenchmarking?

> **Don't reinvent everything—or, rather, only reinvent that small part that will make your product much simpler, more convincing, and more popular. That is enough! But it is also an imperative if you wish to get along.**

1.7 THERE IS LIFE UNDER THE ICE

> *There are no facts, only interpretations.*
> *—Friedrich Nietzsche*

"Everything got frozen. The economy, the businesses, the atmosphere was frozen over," an American businessman said in connection with the 2008 economic crisis. He was obviously right. The economy had slowed down, as everything does during the winter months. But he was wrong in one respect. There *was* life under the ice.

A research institute in Tihany, Hungary, conducted major research to see what happens in winter to the underwater fauna and flora of Lake Balaton. Bigger fish obviously do not die; the carp—grass and silver carp—survive the winter at the deepest points of the lake. The pike keep on eating throughout the winter, moving and hunting under the ice. Antarctica, not famous for its teeming maritime life, surprised researchers, too, when they found relatively developed animal species, including a crablike creature and something resembling a medusa, under a 183-meter-thick layer of ice.

Similarly, there are opportunities concealed by a business crisis—opportunities to make an organization more efficient, to review and optimize procedures, to make quality improvements. True, they are more difficult to find and sometimes extremely painful to implement. But just as the fauna and flora living under the ice adjust to extreme circumstances, so do we, as managers, have to find a solution to things and develop survival techniques for the difficult and chilly period of a crisis.

In my opinion, this is no coincidence. There are no coincidences, anyway—just flip through the pages of Mikhail Bulgakov's *The Master and Margarita* and you will see I am not alone in thinking this. In the plot of that book, Professor Woland, presenting himself sometimes as a black magician and sometimes as a historian-consultant, "forecasts" exactly what is to happen to Berlioz, the editor of a magazine. In a park in 1930s Moscow, a stranger joins in a conversation with Berlioz and Ivan Nikolayevich, a homeless poet:

> "No brick will ever fall on anybody's head just out of the blue. And I can assure you that a brick in no way threatens you. You'll die a different death."
>
> "Perhaps you know what sort exactly?" enquired Berlioz with completely natural irony, getting drawn into an absurd sort of conversation. "And you'll tell me?"
>
> "Readily," responded the stranger. He sized Berlioz up, as though intending to make him a suit, and muttered

under his breath something like: "One, two [...] You'll have your head cut off!"

Homeless goggled with wild, angry eyes at the free-and-easy stranger, while Berlioz asked with a crooked grin:

"By whom, precisely? Enemies? Interventionists?"

"No, by a young Russian woman in the Communist League of Youth."

"Hm ..." mumbled Berlioz, irritated by the stranger's little joke. "Well, excuse me, but that's hardly likely."

Later, it turns out that the stranger—who sometimes introduces himself as this Professor Woland—is Satan himself. Editor Berlioz dies the same night, exactly as the stranger predicted. He slips, because a character, Annushka, had spilled some oil. He falls, and a tram driven by a woman who is in the Communist League of Youth decapitates him. The plot then follows several routes.

As Konstantin Paustovsky wrote of Bulgakov, "The life of this restless and excellent writer was filled with a merciless struggle against stupidity and meanness: a fight for pure human intentions, that this man might be intelligent and noble-spirited because he cannot be anything else. Bulgakov had efficient weapons ..."

Hopefully, as company managers, we will not have to fight against stupidity throughout our lives, but we'll certainly have to struggle to ensure the efficient and successful operations of the company. In this sense, there is no coincidence or chance involved. Of course, everything is relative, and certain situations may redraw one's business options. We know several examples where a company's activity has changed radically over the years. It is no accident either that all major companies interested in petroleum processing have a business-line interested in the utilization of alternative energy sources.

Whether the business environment is favorable or is frozen in ice by the Antarctic cold, you can still be effective if you always have up-to-date information on the global and regional business trends relevant to your company, the target market, and the business risks and opportunities inherent in this, as well as the competitive nature of your resources. If we regularly update such data, we'll know what is happening, and we'll be able to make reasonable estimates as to the tendencies we might expect. Moreover, if you see clearly and understand external processes and are aware of the capabilities of the company, you will also know how to reach your targets.

Results are seldom accidental for those who are always looking for new opportunities.

1.8 THE LEADER AS GARDENER

The test of a manager's suitability is not what performance he is capable of but what his colleagues are capable of without him.
—*W. Steven Brown*

A good gardener knows exactly what plants he needs to care for—yet he knows also that a tree or flower can function and grow without him, so there is no need to be there by its side continuously. He watches its growth and helps to ensure that it will not suffer lack of anything, so it can grow undisturbed. To give it as much water as it needs and as much light as is adequate is all that's necessary. He does not overwater or dry it out; he does not burn it or allow it to wither. He knows exactly at all times what the tree, shrub, or flower in his garden needs. This is how his garden will be beautiful and his plants will flourish. They will feel good in their healthy and natural environment. This is good also for the gardener, who has thus attained his goal.

A manager is just like a good gardener. The organization he supervises would be viable without him—if the boss is on holiday for two weeks, processes will not grind to a halt in his absence. In "nice weather," he performs the "core tasks," supervising and operating the company. He pays no more and no less attention to operations than is necessary. He does not water excessively, but he does not sit back comfortably either; he is on the alert to have ready solutions to problems should a time of crisis come, to enable prompt intervention and ensure the good performance of the organization even in more turbulent times.

He is on guard; he knows what is to be done if the garden is being threatened by a pest or a disease—in this case, if the competition is hunting down high-potential employees or efficient work is being hindered by damaging internal conflicts. The good manager, like the good gardener, welcomes change, for change is his real raison d'être.

The following true war story inspired thoughts like the above for me, although gardening and warfare have little in common. A subordinate of Robert E. Lee, Confederate general in the US Civil War, disregarded a command—and not for the first time—thereby upsetting Lee's plans. The general, who was usually a calm gentleman, lost his temper. When he had calmed down, one of his aides asked him why he did not relieve the disobedient commander of his post. He replied with indignation: "What a question! He wins his battles."

When I received my first managerial commission and became acquainted with my team, it never came to my mind to allocate time to understanding the behavior of the team's members. People were aware of their tasks and goals, so everything would be all right, I thought. Time went by, and not everything turned out as I expected, although I usually worked till late at night. First one team member was in arrears with his task, so I helped him; then another encountered some obstacles. Of course, it also happened that a presentation would be ready on time, but it was full of errors.

After a few months, I was spending even my weekends working with team members, for I insisted that nothing should be delivered that was not impeccable in regard to its materials. Shortly afterward, I came to the conclusion—learned the hard way—that a single person cannot and should not do the tasks of a whole team. The manager has to adjust his team to the task at hand.

I now know that my first efforts looked like (to use a horticultural example) telling the trees in the orchard what yield I expected of them, then breaking down the average yield by tree and not caring for conditions anymore. There was no warming up; hence the "yield" was only what it happened to turn out to be. Attuning the team to a task implies the following three activities by the manager:

1. Alignment of objectives and operational processes
2. Individual motivation
3. Gathering the team together

The manager should optimize the human and material resources available to him. Resources are, in the final analysis, expenses, and since tasks keep changing, it is important that they should be examined and optimized on a regular basis. Operational efficiency can only be developed if the manager comes to a clear understanding of the strengths and weaknesses of his team members and finds the factors that motivate both individuals and the team.

Performance can be maximized by situational and capacity-oriented leadership. There are many motivation tools; their use can be mastered and they can be made use of. Any of them can bring about results, though an honest conversation at least once a year and, if possible, not during working hours, will highlight many things. You just have to listen to the messages.

A classification according to the situational leadership theory espoused by Dr. Paul Hersey and Ken Blanchard is based on whether the employee is willing to perform a task or not and whether he is capable of doing it or not. This model proposes four kinds of task assignments for the four combinations, depending on a team member's willingness and capability to do the task. If the members of the team are motivated, the situation will be much simpler. A motivated team is the best guarantee of successful operations because its members feel as if they are owners of the results, and they experience success together.

General Lee had a capable commander who was headstrong but who won his battles. Nevertheless, the South did not win the war. A single genius was not enough for this, not even then. Neither is a single motivated individual enough in the global economic jungle of the twenty-first century. If the team cannot be amalgamated for a common goal, there will always be points of tension. This, in turn, very efficiently robs the manager of his time. The good gardener knows how to make his garden produce good results.

Do you know how to maximize the performance of your team?

1.9   WHEN SHOULD ONE INTRODUCE CHANGE?

When we least expect it, life sets us a challenge to test our courage and willingness to change; at such a moment, there is no point in pretending that nothing has happened or in saying that we are not yet ready with our decision. The challenge will not wait. Life does not look back.
—*Paulo Coelho,* The Devil and Miss Prym

The perpetuum mobile is a hypothetical machine that, once set in motion, will keep moving endlessly without any additional external energy apart from the one setting it off. To the great grief of researchers, such a thing has not been built yet. However, every field of life is perpetually in motion, at least in the sense that things are changing. We are aware of some events and learn of others when we least expect them. Companies develop new products and services. This is predictable, as opposed to when a known or unknown rival might appear on the market with a new way of doing things.

Many have analyzed and researched Apple's triumphs in recent years. All have focused on the distinctive feature of the Apple way of operating, on the secret of its success, and on what makes its sales increase year after year. Some voted for its special characteristics; others thought the explanation lay in Steve Jobs's charismatic personality. This varied positive feedback may have blinded Apple's management, and it may be the reason why Samsung succeeded in surprising Apple with its new telephones in 2011 and also 2012. Has Apple's monopoly position eroded unexpectedly?

The fight seems to be ongoing. There are lawsuits in progress in several countries initiated by Apple against Samsung. Some of these activities have backfired. The London court did not accept

Apple's argument, and Apple is having to bear the costs of the patent appropriation investigation, which implies free promotion for Samsung. Yet the latest developments have been in favor of Apple. According to the ruling of the court in San Jose, California, Samsung made use of technical innovations from Apple's revolutionary iPhone and iPad equipment. Apple had originally claimed $2.75 billion from Samsung, but the court did not accept all the statements of the company, and the compensation amount was reduced to $1.05 billion.

Samsung also sued Apple for $422 million for patent infringement, but its claims were rejected by the court. Litigation continued for more than a year, and the story isn't over, as the South Korean company has indicated that it will lodge an appeal against the first decision. Samsung stressed in its communiqué that "the decision cannot be regarded as Apple's victory—the losers of the suit are American consumers." In Samsung's opinion, the consequence of the ruling will be less innovation and a more limited selection, while prices will, in all probability, be higher. Apple and Samsung have patent suits pending in several countries, but so far neither has won a walloping victory.

The business world is a nonmechanical perpetuum mobile, so one can expect aggressive actions from competitors at any time. New product design, new technical offerings, new functions, or simply a new fashion—something will certainly happen to upset the relative balance of the market. On such occasions, the cards are reshuffled. The problem is that the marked effects are difficult to calculate in advance, unless it is your own company that is introducing some novelty onto the market. The question is well-justified: when should a company's operations be changed so that it can stand among the winners of the contest?

Apple's example demonstrates that "when to change" is not the right way to ask the question, for it presumes knowledge of a specific time. Yet there is no such time: you cannot tell what rivals may be doing and when (unless you have a James Bond–type agent at your service to collect such valuable information). Consequently, neither can one estimate precisely when an arising problem might be dealt with using available resources. The real question, therefore, is not *when* to change but when *not* to!

An enterprise should keep looking for new solutions but treat them with caution. As Oscar Wilde wrote, "The play was a huge success, but the public is a real catastrophe." That is, even if you perform excellently, the market may still not need what is being offered to it.

Continual development is therefore the first and foremost task of the leader. The key to long-term, efficient, and effective company operations is the development of competitiveness. It is irrelevant whether it is a small or medium-sized enterprise or a global multinational company—every entity has rivals, and each one is influenced by economic conditions and market trends. A boss will always have to lead the company he is directing to success in a perpetually moving environment.

For more than twenty years now, consumer habits have been interwoven throughout our lives. Markets were opened up in the early 1990s, and the technical commodities market, too, was characterized as having new outlets and lowering prices. At that time, a story like this one from German relatives seemed strange and almost unbelievable:

> If a television or coffee machine breaks down, we don't waste much time—we get rid of it on the occasion of a clear-out. I remember that even at the end of the 1990s, we calculated with two-digit inflation; yet the price of technical articles did not change—it did not increase. If one's coffee machine broke down, it cost around 5,000 forints to have it repaired; while a new one with a warranty cost hardly 10 percent more than this. So we bought a new one, and the old one landed in the garbage can.

Not even thirty years ago, an electrician's qualification was more precious than gold—it was clean work with little in the way of physical stress, and good earnings. What has become of that market? Today, color TVs, washing machines, and the like all come to the same fate: if they are obsolete or if they break down, you get rid of them and buy a new one. I'm quite sure that the number of workers making their living repairing technical products is only a tenth of what it used to be in the nineties.

Since it is impossible to avoid change, we live in an environment that is perpetually in motion—where successful companies are the ones where the management does its best to grasp the new opportunities produced by change and to deter any risk effects. Products and services should be developed continuously, whereas product introductions and operational changes should be phased in and also adjusted to the rhythm of the market. Always have new developments in store; and as to their conversion into cash, make that a part of your tactic.

Be always one step ahead of your rivals.

1.10 RESTRUCTURING: ON WHAT BASIS?

Meditation is the death of action.
—Imre Madách

Globalization multiplies the size of accessible markets. Besides their own conquered market positions, where it may be more difficult to grow, companies of course exploit every opportunity to expand their exports. That may trigger more intensive growth. Growth, however, redraws demand, and the regional forces change. Sooner or later, internal corporate processes will get overloaded and will need to be reorganized. If this is omitted, competitiveness will slowly be curtailed.

On such occasions it may happen that the products and services can only reach the consumer via the logic of logistics, in a roundabout way, traveling much more than necessary; or that products are not fully compliant with the market expectations of the destination country, so that their adjustment will impose *a posteriori* extra costs. Export-market expansion, initially an option, will slowly become a hindrance if no development takes place. The solution in such cases is efficiency enhancement or expansion, though up to a certain point only, since this, too, has its limits. If growth has reached a critical level in terms of sales complexity, there is no other solution but development—a reconsidering of business processes while taking note of, if possible, the foreseeable demand.

In connection with the reorganization of processes, let me highlight two errors that occur rather frequently, in my opinion. The first makes me think of the saying of the Sicilian writer Giuseppe Tomasi di Lampedusa: "If you want things to stay the same, they are going to have to change." Unfortunately, a manager who is driven by a desire to prove himself sometimes does not think of this. In highly exceptional cases, if everything in the reorganization turns out as planned, this might not be a problem. However, as I have mentioned, this is not typical at all of projects affecting large organizations and also operational procedures. If, on the other hand, there is a delay, a capable manager is needed who will be able to determine where to interfere to keep the process under control.

Just imagine a car in which the display signals and the pedals have been moved around. Nothing is where it had been. Without time to learn where each item had been moved to, would you dare take a ride with it on the highway? And if you had a choice between two cars, one that is driven in the usual way and this new one, which would you get into if you had to be on your way somewhere at once? Into the old one, wouldn't you, to take no risks? An enterprise works in the same way, which is why Lampedusa's saying rings so true.

The second error generally occurs in the context of product or service development, when you forget that the developmental phase or lead time before going onto the market ("time to market") determines to a significant degree to what extent the product will meet market requirements. Let's assume that the product or service adheres exactly to the requirements defined by the market research but, for some reason, the decision is suspended in the development phase. What then? The requirements and the deadlines are known, but a decision or funding has to be waited for.

The crisis caused many serious liquidity problems for many firms, but important projects tend to be decelerated rather than cancelled in such cases. Or it may happen that the project focus changes slightly, that the list of requirements is extended or an unexpected difficulty occurs. If no extra resources are available, time pressure appears. This has its limits, however, and the time to market or lead time will certainly deteriorate.

It is a natural response in such cases for a project team to handle only the criteria that it has to. It is in possession of the already acquired and valid licenses. If blockage causes too much delay, by the time the project is brought to fruition, it may be sufficient for the approved purposes, yet there is a high chance that market needs will have already changed.

The success of the product or service is significantly influenced by timing—that is, the time to market, which is the time needed to make the product or service accessible relative to the project's commencement. In a market where tendencies may alter markedly every twelve to eighteen months, project implementation must not be prolonged to thirty-six months. Imagine the success of a mobile-phone manufacturer who attempted to conquer customers with a "new" mobile phone that had been in fashion three years earlier.

To avoid such situations, it is recommended to include the time-to-market parameter in any target specification. Restructuring and development are necessary, but to be successful, one must not forget that implementation inevitably takes place in a changing environment. That is, the implementation timetable needs to be designed with expected modifications coming from the environment being taken into consideration. And, of course, plan according to your resources or you will get a grip on a lot yet retain little.

Everything changes, even the basis on which one designs new products.

1.11 MAKE YOUR DECISION, HERE AND NOW

A certain number of failures is indispensable for success. If you have never been unsuccessful, that merely shows that you have set yourself excessively safe objectives, and you haven't tested yourself sufficiently to be able to develop.
—*David Viscott*

Aldous Huxley's protagonist in his book *Island* is shipwrecked on a rockbound coast. He loses consciousness but fortunately drifts to shore, where he is awakened by a strange bird yelling "Here and now, boys, here and now." And the mynah bird continues, "Here and now!" The protagonist is a British journalist, landing by chance on an exotic island-state, one isolated from the world. The inhabitants of the island save his life, and while he is recovering, they show him their happy country combining the advantages of Eastern and Western civilization. The utopian story continues as it depicts a totally disillusioned, cynical British journalist becoming a happy and wise island reform-thinker, capable of everything and in particular of surpassing his former self for a just cause.

From our point of view, the crucial thing is the mynah bird, which is "like the electric light … They don't belong to anybody" and keeps repeating "Here and now." Make your decision, here and now! To the journalist's inquiry as to why the bird says those things, the explanation is, "That's what you always forget, isn't it? I mean, you forget to pay attention to what's happening. And that's the same as not being here and now."

But let's return from Pala, the fantasy island, to reality. The message of the mynah bird may be useful. Unless you pay attention to what's actually happening and make your decision at the right time, you will merely drift with events. And if you do that as the leader of a company, your company will also do nothing but drift like a forsaken ship on the sea.

I remember a case at our company. Sanyi had joined the firm two years before. After a short trial period, he was appointed logistics manager. The first year passed in relative calm, with minor operational problems, but he had a good team and his fellow managers accepted him. He thought he had made a good choice, and work colleagues agreed.

The new year set in with a new project. Significant volume growth had to be attained. Over barely ten months, the production volume had to be doubled without any increase in inventory. At the same time, of course, clients needed to be served on time, just as before. The tense pace, the tight deadline, and the sometimes scarce resources caused many disputes at management meetings. Then, as the tasks kept piling up, the situation became critical. Incoming materials were stored in the courtyard because they hadn't been entered into the books. Packaging materials were drenched by rain, so production could only keep up with orders with overtime and delays; and as might be expected, the phones were ringing ever more frequently as customers prompted us to fulfill their orders.

No one understood what was happening, nor did Sanyi for a while. The situation was analyzed regularly at the weekly meetings, where he presented the problems encountered in the logistics field and anticipated consequences. He said what he could do by himself and what required joint decision-making. Józsi, the production foreman, also supplied information, which he'd assessed and classified from his own perspective. There was no problem so long as managers took measures within their own fields. However, as a result of operating mechanisms being burdened by the many changes, problems affected several areas at once, and they continued to proliferate. These ought to have been decided upon "here and now," when they were discussed. However, because of data deficiencies and most often to contradictory proposals and opinions, no decisions were taken at the management meetings.

The second year passed, and Sanyi got fed up. He resigned. "Even a bad decision taken there and then, when you are analyzing a problem, is better than no decision at all," he said upon parting. Maybe the local managers needed this to snap them out of their slumber. The firm lost a good professional, but the team managed to correct the defective procedure in time.

Of course, one could think of many possible reasons why a manager might fail to decide upon an issue. Perhaps he doesn't notice that decision-making cannot be postponed any longer and he should act, irrespective of the available information. Or perhaps he doesn't pay heed to what is happening here and now. Or maybe he does recognize how grave the situation is, but he is simply unable to make a decision. From the point of view of outcome, the specific cause is irrelevant.

It is important to decide in time.

1.12 HOW MUCH IS THE STRATEGY WORTH?

*If you want to build a ship, don't drum up the men to
gather wood, divide the work, and give orders. Instead,
teach them to yearn for the vast and endless sea.*
—*Antoine de Saint-Exupéry*

I cannot say that *Alice's Adventures in Wonderland* was my favorite childhood reading; on the contrary, when I first came across it at the age of eight, I didn't even read it through—I did not understand it and I was bored by it. Nonetheless, I will now quote from it, because I myself could not put what I want to say more eloquently. Alice stood at a crossroad in Wonderland. Startled by seeing the Cheshire Cat sitting on a bough of a tree a few yards off, she asked it:

> "Would you tell me, please, which way I ought to go from here?"
>
> "That depends a good deal on where you want to get to," said the Cat.
>
> "I don't much care where—" said Alice.
>
> "Then it doesn't matter which way you go," said the Cat.

Are strategy and objectives important for a company? The answer, the essence, could not be summed up better than by acknowledging what the Cheshire Cat said. If you know where you want to get to, it is not irrelevant at all which direction you should go, or what to do and how to do things to reach your destination.

The bigger a company, the more energy it allocates to the development of various charters, codes, and strategies. I have the impression that the big ones maybe more than is necessary, and the small ones less than might be required. However, the Cheshire Cat's retort is quite clear. You have to know the answer to the question of where you want to get to.

If you have no goal, you can go any way; yet if you do have one, it will show you the right direction, in the same way as a lighthouse guides a ship. In the context of globalization and intensifying market competition, it is even better if each and every employee is aware of the goal. If such objectives can be made the desired personal goals of all individuals concerned, this is guarantee enough for the common efforts being made to attain the objectives.

Express the objectives in an understandable way and make them accessible to all. Make your message short, concise, and comprehensible. The employees should know where the "ship" that they are on is heading. They have to know how to make decisions, as appropriate, to promote the effective and efficient activities of their company. If this is achieved, make recognition a lasting experience, in acknowledgement of the fun of teamwork; if it is not achieved, there will be no feelings of shared happiness over the company's successes either.

It is important to make it known to both employees and business partners, or even the broad strata of society, why the company was formed, what long-term objectives it has set itself, and what values it has opted for. It is not sufficient solely to indicate the goal; the desire for it and the joys associated with it must also be awakened. Let it be a positive memory to all if objectives are met. If they are motivating, if people adopt them and the experience of shared success after a successful period of time warms their hearts, it is only then that they can be expected to undertake any extra work (voluntary overtime, for example, perhaps a call to a customer outside business hours if a problem occurs, or collaboration over the weekend to help each other out) that will make the company more permanently successful.

This is why I chose Antoine de Saint-Exupéry's words to start this section. If a leader manages to raise the desire of the crew to attain certain goals, no greater guarantee is needed for setting out on the path of implementation with confidence. You may have a dream, but you have to dream with the team to be certain of success.

In the early nineties, the managers of a small electronics office-equipment company had a dream. The opening up of the economy had created new opportunities both domestically and in neighboring countries. This encouraged them to expand their activities. Since at that time it was possible to acquire massive stocks of secondhand office equipment at an incredibly low price, it seemed a good idea to sell those in Romania and in the Ukraine.

The company repaired and sold electrical office technology. Its business strategy was built on long-term customer relationships. "We guarantee the operation and, if necessary, the replacement of office equipment. You can concentrate on your core activity," the managers told their business partners. The employees were not salesmen but, basically, technical staff and technicians; yet regular client contact and smooth repair services built very strong bonds, so much so that the company won 99 percent of the electrical office-equipment tenders from its former domestic customers.

For the foreign markets, the management set only sales objectives. They assumed that the technology that had already been replaced in the West would remain marketable and easy to sell at a sufficiently low price for a long time in the East. However, there were several errors in their calculations. First of all, they did not take into consideration the repair-service requirements for the products concerned, which they could not satisfy. The biggest problem, however, was that there was no team abroad to accept and also adopt their objectives and their ideas to achieve them. The people they hired were temporary staff.

The export manager of the electrical office-equipment company abandoned the business model that was a success at home and focused on sales alone in a mostly unknown and transforming market. The company had objectives, but not sufficiently elaborate ones, and the team members focused on their own welfare, not on the goals. I think I will not be revealing any secrets if I say that they were only able to sell a single container of goods abroad.

The failure had three main causes. The first two have already been mentioned. The third is a strategic error: they failed to note that in a transforming economy, everyone is looking for modern products and new ways of doing things. People in the countries lying to the east of Hungary had also had enough of secondhand items that were difficult to operate. This way of thinking determined to a large extent the decisions of the nineties.

It is the task and responsibility of the manager to define smart goals. SMART is also the acronym for the following attributes of the smart goal:

- specific
- measurable
- attainable
- realistic
- timely

Don't forget that successful implementation also requires a pinch of longing in the team to accomplish goals.

Implementation shows the value of our strategy.

1.13 THE TIGER'S FUR

If you want things to really change, you need different thoughts.
—*Abraham Hicks*

Imagine: a scientist called Alan Turing realized in 1952 that biological patterns in nature, such as the tiger's stripes, are the result of so-called morphogenic interactions. Morphogenes regulate tissue development by signal transmission molecules. According to Turing, the development of the patterns is due to an activator and inhibitor pair. The activators are responsible for the development of the tiger's dark stripes, and the inhibitors prevent the spread of the dark color over the entire body surface. So the striped fur of the tiger is the result of the complementary activity and alternation of the activators and inhibitors.

Turing was an excellent and versatile scientist, but tigers are not interested in this theory. Most live in forests and grasslands, and the pattern of their fur helps them adapt to their environment and hide themselves from their prey. The alternating black and orange stripes may be striking at first sight, but they are exactly what ensure the tiger's concealment in the dry and yellowish grass.

To me, the tiger's fur is a metaphor for the diversity of life and identifying possibilities. Active and passive, good and bad periods alternate in our lives, just as stripes do on a tiger's fur. You have to find opportunities in this alternation. At the time of the onset of the economic crisis at the end of 2008, no one thought that in 2012 we would not be thinking of it as past history. Many analyses have been and still are being released along with many alarming predictions on the effects of the crisis.

This makes me think of the joke in which a few shipwrecked Hungarian sailors have been lying on a boat that has been upside down for days. They are without food and drink utterly exhausted. Suddenly, one of them cries out, "Ha-jó, ha-jó" (this is a pun: in Hungarian, *hajó* in one word means "ship," but in two words *ha jó* is "if I [verb] well"), at which the others jump into the water to swim to the ship. "If I see it well, there are sharks coming," the stuttering man finishes his warning. News about an arriving ship seemed good at first, and the others believed it, even though the idea may have crossed their mind that they'd better look around before taking it for granted.

There was a flood of negative news in relation to the economic crisis, and, willy-nilly, our reaction was quite similar to that of the sailors. The prognoses, pessimistic and even more pessimistic ones that were heard at various forums, got into our heads, and we gradually came to believe that we were/are in great trouble. However, instead of panicking, we ought to have focused on solutions. Don't forget: life is like the tiger's fur, sometimes dark, in other places light. We are facing more or less favorable conditions, but the leader's task is to focus on the solution to problems in both cases. Don't draw far-reaching conclusions from—and base your decisions on—half words and inadequate information. Don't let a business crisis evolve into a confidence crisis. You might rightfully ask why a confidence crisis has to evolve.

In his book *Influence: Science and Practice*, Robert B. Cialdini asks if there is anyone who likes the laugh track on TV programs. All respondents said it was stupid and utterly superfluous. Nevertheless, producers have kept on using it. It has been shown in experiments that under the effects of positive reactions to such "laughter," the viewer also laughs more often and for a longer time, and deems the program more humorous. This actually relates to the theorem of social proof based on similar empirical observations. According to this principle, people often seek to find out what others believe and do in situations similar to theirs to be able to decide what to believe and how to behave themselves, and they proceed accordingly. The social-proof principle might also be used to persuade someone to make a certain decision. If you can make him believe that many others have acted in a similar way, he will follow suit.

Research has helped us define two situations where the principle of social proof has an extraordinary effect: one is uncertainty, and the other is similarity. Of all models, people are most happy to follow the behavioral example of peers. This is deadly serious, as shown by the suicide-statistic analyses of David Phillips, sociologist at San Diego University. The analyses demonstrate that after a suicide case is given wide media coverage, there is a high number of suicides by people whose situation, age, and other characteristics are very similar to the victim in the headlines. Phillips calls this the "Werther effect."

The label comes from the novel *The Sorrows of Young Werther*, which made its author, the outstanding German writer J. W. Goethe, an overnight success more than two hundred years ago. At that time, the novel and the suicide of the protagonist, the young Werther, had a great impact on readers and triggered a wave of copycat suicides throughout Europe. The principle of social proof is based on such mass reactions. In the opinion of Cialdini, responsiveness to false social proofs can be reduced effectively by recognizing their falseness, and this will automatically disengage the mechanism of people's automatic copying of the model.

One may complain about its being either light or dark—that is, that events occur within the context of the orange or the black stripe—but this will be to little avail. If you pay excessive attention to analyzing specific situations, uncertainty will end up influencing an ever broader area of society, and given the principle of social proof, it will be much more difficult to overcome such situations.

Instead of risks and a desperate situation, managers should speak more about the issues—and the press should not merely echo the concerns but, instead, cover solutions and the efforts needed to attain a goal. Otherwise, we will have to pay a double price for recovery from a crisis. However difficult the situation, focus on the solution.

And, apropos the tiger, Gábor Pesthy's article in *Origo*, "Did the Tigers Make a Wise Decision?" is about their accommodation capacity. According to a survey conducted in a national park in Nepal, the tigers there shifted to nocturnal life in order to have fewer conflicts with men. Neil Carter, a PhD student at Michigan State University, studied with his colleagues the tigers of Chitwan National Park, Nepal, for two years. They installed motion-sensitive camera "traps," analyzed the tigers' prey, and also noted the movement of people on the roads and paths of the national park. Under normal circumstances, tigers move about by both day and night. On the site under study, however, Carter and his colleagues discovered that the tigers turned into nocturnal animals. Apparently, their wisdom had solved the problem existing in the park.

> **Risks are omnipresent, yet the essential thing is a solution to them, so leaders should emphasize the solutions. Show the way out.**

1.14 NEED LUCK?

> *If a man does not know to what port he is steering,*
> *no wind will be favorable to him.*
> —*Seneca*

In regard to business processes and opportunities, I have always defined them as aspects of a cycle. In response to changing effects, we will keep seeking out new solutions to issues, planning and implementing ideas, and enjoying the outcomes of our work. Then the cycle repeats itself, in just the same way as the seasons follow one another.

Autumn creates a new situation, and the options then change. In wintertime, you gather your strength, make preparations, and nourish new ideas. Spring is the time of doing, of execution, the season of strength regenerated. Summer is the time of harvesting, of gathering the crop, and of a well-earned rest for all. Then everything starts anew.

This business cycle may move along a positive spiral if it is sustainable and creative in nature, or follow a downward, negative spiral (unfortunately) if you cannot find the right direction. Good targets are needed to keep the enterprise on the positive spiral course, yet chance and luck may also be of help to us at times. Yet how important are the latter? How much do they influence outcomes? This question is open to debate: you may believe in luck or deny its role completely. Let everyone decide for himself or herself how important luck or a correct choice of target really is.

I would like to share two stories with the reader in this connection. One is an anecdote; the other is a story from personal experience.

The first is about the famous nuclear physicist Niels Bohr, who loved hunting. His friends and fellow hunters often visited Bohr's hunting lodge, which had an enormous horseshoe fixed above the entrance gate. A colleague asked him once at the hunters' dinner table, "You don't believe in this luck thing, do you?"

"I don't," Bohr said, "but it does work."

The second story is of something that happened to me twenty-one years ago. Despite my relatively fresh engineering degree and strong love for my profession, I switched to marketing in 1991. I foresaw many opportunities inherent in the combination of the dynamic development of information technology and economic changes. After a short spell of work experience, I applied for the marketing director's job at a large public enterprise. This was a brave undertaking, as I had arrived in Hungary with "a single suitcase" and my family only two years earlier. A long nine months followed, including a series of assessments, psychological testing, and interviews.

There were only three candidates left by the end of the year when something unexpected happened: a privatization contract for the company was signed. When I was invited to an interview in January 1993 together with the other two remaining candidates, we met representatives of the new owner. This was followed by several interviews in the next two months.

Finally, the president of the company told me the following: "We're going to fill the marketing director's job with someone who knows the products manufactured by the new owners. You don't. Yet, in our opinion, your qualifications, competencies, and experience make you suitable for directing the three-year project to restructure the company, and we would like to delegate that to you, provided that you agree."

I was surprised, and also a little sad, because I had wanted so much to win the position of marketing director. After some hesitation, I said okay. It did not take long to realize that, despite every initial difficulty, I had made a good decision. The restructuring of a public company and its integration into the operations of an international group was an excellent learning opportunity. Furthermore, it meant an opportunity to gain international experience, as my later work offered me an insight into—and even a chance to participate in—the activities of various foreign companies.

Seven years later, our president retired, and at the farewell dinner organized in his honor we happened to be alone at the dinner table for a short time. He said, "I still remember our first meeting at the firm. You know, your application interview. Well, I thought then that in '56 I set out from Hungary to the Big World as you did in '90 from Romania. At that time, someone helped me start my career in France. This is why I decided to hire you, because you reminded me of my former self, and I also wanted to give someone an opportunity—but it was up to you to grasp it!"

Certainly, sometimes you do not even notice things, and realize only in retrospect that there and then you had been lucky. I have thought of this man with respect to this day.

The essential thing is to have goals and, with perseverance, to realize them. Luck will also find you sooner or later.

1.15   GUEST STORY

Choice of the Strategy-Making Approach at an Institution of Higher Education

Márton Villmányi
University of Szeged
Dean of the Faculty of Economics

My thoughts laid out below will lead the reader to a field that is far from being considered a model example of market competition, to my homeland in the narrow sense, and to the waters of strategy-making at institutions of higher education. The example may be surprising or just interesting, but it is nevertheless worth quoting a nonprofit organization as an example of change, orientation, and accommodation to highlight the idea that the experiences described above are not sector- or business-specific but represent core issues within organizational management.

Let me lead the reader away from the topical issues that, although they do offer examples and models in abundance, are maybe less demonstrative of wise judgment, and step back to the maelstrom of the mid-2000s, which shows a picture similar to the chaotic one of our days, albeit for different reasons. In the mid-2000s, higher education institutions (HIEs) were facing what seemed an enormous task at that time. The financial and organizational integration of the universities and colleges into large regional institutions (with a budget of HUF 30–50 billion) had come to an end on January 1, 2000, and they had to launch steps for content integration—that is, they had to take on board the "Bologna process," the end result of European-level conventions.

The introduction of the most spectacular component, two-level education, could not be postponed any longer; at the same time, student enrollment had reached its peak and made the organizations concerned come face to face with an unprecedented workload in Hungary. Aware of these changes, the administration submitted a bill designed to reregulate this sector to Parliament, while expecting a radical reform of the HIEs.

Let me mention, to indicate the complexity of the situation, that the program for European development and preparation of the second National Development Plan had also started meanwhile. Participation in the preparation of the NDP was not only in the best interests of the institutions themselves (by giving them an opportunity to enforce their own concepts in the national planning process), it was also an aspect of their social responsibility. The professional capacities on show at universities and colleges and people's confidence in their unbiased nature often appeared as a key issue during regional or branch-level planning.

At the University of Szeged, where my story takes place, change was obvious at every level. Created through the merger of five predecessor institutions on January 1, 2000, the USZ is one of the biggest of the Hungarian HIEs. At that time, it had eleven faculties and an annual budget of HUF 50 billion (of which the normative educational/academic state support was HUF 20 billion); 30,000 students took courses there, and the university employed 6,500 people. In 2003–2004, it became clear to the institution's management that without a strategy that was known and supported by both internal stakeholders and external partners, the changes might not occur or could be derailed; and this is not to speak of the assertion of a need deriving from the core striving of HIEs in which maintenance of academic and teaching excellence represents but an acceptable minimum.

There were many open issues. Goals were needed, yet what should they be? And how does one specify objectives that external partners can understand and get to know and that internal stakeholders can identify with? How to treat in a balanced way fields with very different natures, like education research, and other services within the institution? How to ensure flexibility of strategy while keeping an eye on development priorities—knowing that, for example, it takes eight to fifteen years for a field of higher education to develop itself, while its appearance as a place of research reaching international standards takes even longer and will cost billions of forints? How does one ensure that the strategy will be the point of departure for the allocation of development funds and the operative implementation of developmental priorities? How can strategy become a means for the implementation of changes and of accommodation?

The answer was simple: you need a plan. Which triggered another question: just one plan? Is it possible to integrate into a plan designed from a single point of view the answer to the great questions of life and death, of the world, to agree on it and to break it down into subunits so that it is understood by partners while bearing in mind that the managers of the institution are specialists of their own fields, in the positive sense, and hence do not necessarily understand cost–benefit analyses, activity–base costing, performance management, process management, and the rest? The answer to the second question turned out to be no. By integrating everything into one plan, you would be degrading the essence of strategy-making to the level of document-editing. Yet strategy-making includes understanding our expectations for the future and the characteristics that will shape them, the creation of a vision and goals, a conceptual specification of principal intervention areas, detection of and forecasting of the dynamics of change, and the engagement of key actors.

Instead of a single plan, the university has developed multiple plans, concepts, and approaches. The starting point was formulation of a guiding concept by this "innovative university," a work-group set up by the rector and the institution from among former institution heads representing the fields and branches of science and who have had major successes from both domestic and European perspectives. The work-group reviewed the baseline situation and the main scenarios regarding expectations for the future, and they defined goals, priorities, and developmental alternatives that the university management then put out for consultation with the university's external stakeholders and with organizational units from the institution at official university forums, highlighting milestones and the orders of magnitude of the investments and expenditures involved.

Nevertheless, despite its many attractive features, the concept had endless shortcomings. It was not specific, not suitable for monitoring; it provided no specific clues to implement details; and it did not explain the respective activities of units and individuals. The institution made an attempt to transform the concept into a detailed operational plan. This did not work. It was sophisticated and chaotic—even the designers themselves failed to understand it at times.

Nine topics were worked out with the contribution of persons involved in their management or coordination to facilitate a breakdown:

1. Educational portfolio
2. Educational structure
3. Educational methodology
4. Basic R+D+I profiles
5. Research support
6. R+D+I utilization
7. Service portfolio
8. Service development
9. Institution management

The educational strategy was worked out via the positioning approach used with strategy-making, by optimizing the weight of the educational activity of the institution in the various educational fields and looking at the relevant labor market demand. The R+D+I strategy was developed under the resource-based approach to strategy-making; to specify the guidelines, institutional R+D+I competencies as well as the necessary investments, specific sites, and orders of magnitude for developments were determined. Because of the intense market competition, the complexity of the services, and the very short development deadline, the service strategy was formulated through the learning approach, with special emphasis given to flexible implementation of developments and a fast back-channeling of implementation experiences.

One task remained: to transform all this into a living system, to make it, as the textbooks say, the everyday issue of management/organizational management—and to make change a strategy-oriented and deliberate form of activity. The university adapted a method from the United States for this purpose, hoping that "twisting the indicators" would bring it closer to everyday life. It did not. The relevant organizational, cultural, and IT bases were lacking. The indicators had many advantages (awareness of the facts and their situation, tangible objectives, etc.) but they failed to prompt the participants into action. All this had been done via human experience—firsthand experiences of accepting success or failure and joint evaluations of them.

The institution found that it did have a model already adapted to its needs in each organizational unit and each intervention area, whether concerning quality assurance or process development, or realization of corporate research centers (the list could be continued endlessly). The presentation of experiences, their joint evaluation, and the specification of the development options are strong motivators in themselves, and if they could be supplemented by resources and coordination capacity, they would become successful developments almost from the word go.

Implementation of the strategy can be deemed a success. The institution has made operational 80 percent of the specified targets, and the remaining 20 percent were either swept away by the crisis emerging in 2008 or the organization was not sufficiently prepared for their delivery. In my opinion, however, this only makes the example more illustrative. It is not sufficient to merely understand a situation, namely that change must be brought about—we need to also understand ourselves, our motives, our drivers, and the organizational patterns that we apply in the course of changes. Change and accommodation are never the sole answers, a single development or modification realized by one well-targeted decision—they are, rather, an organic chain of answers and a systemic application of the process of understanding, intervention, experience, and learning.

There is no single solution to this process, no need to place a bet on the red or the black of the roulette table where we have a 50 percent probability. Let's accept the world as being as colorful as it is, with its shades representing so many opportunities. At times of change, too, man is the key organizational resource: only he can alter his way of thinking and conduct, keep reinterpreting the situation and what lies ahead, and support all this by action. Consequently, I sincerely believe that he is the true driver of the organization's successful adaptation to change.

CHAPTER 2

Winter: Looking for Solutions

2.1 A FABLE WITH PENGUINS

Everyone thinks of changing the world,
but no one thinks of changing himself.
—Leo Tolstoy

Who would think that the life of an Antarctic penguin colony could be so revealing about how we react to change? *Our Iceberg Is Melting*, a fable written by John Kotter, brings to light a lot about the topic. A group of Emperor penguins have lived their everyday lives on a floating iceberg for generations. One day, however, one of them starts to notice some environmental changes, the warming and melting that can potentially devastate their homes and the iceberg. Some believe in the signs but others have doubts, which makes it hard to make a decision. Is there a realistic danger, or has one of the penguins misinterpreted the situation? Disputes—sometimes quarrels—lead to a solution being arrived at, followed by action.

If change management is part of your everyday tasks, you will find this an intriguing and illuminating story. The main characters— Fred, Alice, Louis, Buddy, Professor, and NoNo—resemble our acquaintances, or perhaps even us. To be able to adjust to new conditions, we have to make changes. This will only work if we first break away from old habits and change our routine problem-solving strategies—in other words, if we first change ourselves. This may be the hardest part.

The story of the penguin colony is about the fight against change and about heroic deeds as well as clever tactics that might enable us to overcome seemingly unconquerable obstacles. If we move on from the fact that, here, the plot develops on an iceberg, we might find the everyday life of a company embedded in the story. There are the everyday problems of employees, like diminishing respect, being insensitive to the concerns of others, or differences in value as a result of the generation gap. However, changes can take place at a company as well that will entirely rewrite the operational rules— just as in the story, where the change comes because some of the penguins recognize changing trends. Many, however, do not believe that something unalterable might happen in the future, which could be a catastrophe if people are not prepared. A familiar situation, isn't it?

It is not only difficulties created by the economic depression that we need to think of here, for history has demonstrated many situations that created new opportunities while terminating others. Change is part of our lives. It makes a difference, however, whether it happens as part of a process of evolution or revolution—whether we get used to the effects gradually or we have to face up to them suddenly. Whichever way it happens, it is good to have a few tricks up our sleeve to handle the situation. If we follow guidelines and carry out tasks correctly, we can successfully recover from such difficult circumstances. And not only do we adapt ourselves to new developments in this way, we can also keep insecurities caused by the change at bay.

Kotter's change-management approach assists the Emperor penguins. The conflict-resolution methods presented in the book and the practice of handling "frozen" beliefs demonstrate that with effective communication and conscious management of processes and operations, insecurity can be overcome. The book also shows us that change is not the personal affair of the manager but something that concerns everybody, and to make it work every member of the group will have to become involved—especially if we want a permanent result and not merely a swift victory. The book is worth reading, as the fable teaches the reader a great working method as well.

From a manager's point of view, sticking to the following steps provides maximum security when handling an emerging situation:

1. Regular evaluation of technological, economic and social processes, and trend analyses
2. Changes in the target market, the activities of the competition, and the expected impact of trends
3. Preparation for decision-making by involving the accountable members of the group
4. Making a decision about objectives and the changes affecting performance
5. Giving information about scheduled objectives and implementation procedures to those concerned
6. Regular inspection of the implementation process, and evaluation of accomplished sub-objectives
7. Celebration of significant achievements
8. Finalizing the restructuring process and the operations of the new system, and making corrections

Organizing and managing the first four steps is the responsibility of the manager. You have to keep your eyes peeled to be able to find the right solution in an unexpected situation, and you need to be alert so that you can be well prepared. The aim is to comprehend the dangers—and opportunities—as soon as possible, so that you can then prepare for things. Managers have to observe the financial processes along with external and internal trends in much the same way. The further ahead we can count on a reliable forecast, the sooner we can make restructuring plans and look at their implementation. Good timing is the key to success.

When the information we need to have has reached the required level, we have to make a decision. We must decide what, how, and when we are going to change, and who will be able to do this by exploiting the possibilities and avoiding the effects of risk factors the changes may bring about. This does not mean rewriting existing and operational business procedures immediately. The decision we have made means that we will be dealing with existing business processes while it is still worth it and while we still haven't invested in new resources. We have to concentrate resources on the new procedures, the implementation of changes, and reorganization.

The point of the fifth step is to provide accurate information. Those concerned need to know what and why we are doing things like this and what concerns them. Of course, not everyone needs to know the minutest details, but the key to successful implementation of changes is to inform those concerned about the objectives so that they can understand and identify with them as much as possible right from the beginning. The sixth step involves regular evaluation, examining the implementation of changes, handling ideas related to making amendments, and also making decisions and reassessments.

When implementing a major change, there is always passive opposition (those opposing out of habit) and active opposition (those who truly do not believe in the need for change). The more people accept and embrace new objectives and the need for change, the less effect the opposition will have. This is one of the reasons the seventh step—celebrating the achievement of a significant partial result as a mutual success—is so important. It is a piece of evidence, and it means we are heading in the right direction and have successfully closed a chapter. All this reduces the number and influence of opposition members of the team.

Certainly, finalizing the project only happens when we have achieved our objectives—the eighth step. This is the time to examine how close we are to the original plan in regard to achieving our goals, whether we still have to make alterations, or whether we are on the right, new track. Naturally, you must not forget that the way of proceeding developed will only serve as an answer to the business changes for a certain period of time, so after the eighth step—or sooner, if the introductory phase of the changes takes longer than a year—you will need to start all over again with the initial steps.

Change is not hard to follow but to foresee.

2.2   WHO ARE WE IN ACTUAL FACT?

Some walks you have to take alone.
—Suzanne Collins

In the summer of 1990, J. K. Rowling spent a great deal of travel time on the train from Manchester to London. On one of those rail journeys, the thought sprang up in her mind of a boy who was a wizard but didn't know it. As her imagination spun the tale, this young wizard headed off to attend a school of witchcraft and wizardry. By the time she stepped off the train at King's Cross Station, many of the characters and locations of Harry Potter's world and the plot of what would become the first novel in the series were already mapped out in her head. The first edition of *Harry Potter and the Philosopher's Stone* was released in 1997, and phenomenal success led to the film *Harry Potter and the Sorcerer's Stone* (from the book's US title) and many books and movies to follow.

Some people consider the Harry Potter books to be the best and others the worst series of the century. Several psychologists, however, agree that these books are great for improving self-knowledge. I am not competent to make any judgment here—nevertheless, I do strongly feel that there are certain well-founded thoughts in the books that may contain relevant messages for characters in the business world.

When Harry Potter met Dumbledore, the great wizard, for the first time, to Harry he was only the unreachable headmaster of Hogwarts. Their first conversation took place when Harry was walking around the castle in the middle of the night. Dumbledore, instead of giving a warning, sat on the floor beside the young boy and gave him his first lecture, about the magical power of love. This solicitude determined Harry's further development at the wizarding school. A confidential relationship slowly developed between Harry Potter and Dumbledore, who besides being headmaster was the leader of the Order of the Phoenix. One time, when Harry shared with his teacher his excruciating doubts about himself and his ability in wizard magic, as well as his fears of how his abilities had taken a wrong turn, Dumbledore replied with a notable thought: "It is our choices, Harry, that show what we truly are, far more than our abilities."

I would like to draw this to the attention of all managers. It means nothing how professionally such persons delegate or how well they manage time—these abilities by themselves will not make a good manager. The question is how and for what purpose they utilize their knowledge, how they act and decide. Because, as it is put by another Harry Potter character, Sirius Black, "We've all got both light and dark inside us. What matters is the part we choose to act on. That's who we really are." Of course, to make sensible decisions, we have to have adequate self-knowledge and unfaltering values. What do you think?

When I was first appointed as a manager, I was the only member of the management team who did not have a partnership share. The enterprise was mainly privately owned, but a small proportion was still in the public interest, which meant no difficulties in carrying out one's everyday tasks, of course. Besides the managing director and the business manager, there were three of us on the management team, responsible for three different branches of business. My colleagues had already been working at the company for years in similar positions. They were considered to be experienced leaders. I delivered a fresh drive and thousands of new ideas to the team, so we had lots of debates about what to implement and how. We asked questions like, "Is it worth it?" and "How much is it possible to take on?" These debates were beneficial; we chiseled and shaped our ideas and, of course, learned from each other.

I felt really happy at the end of the first year. It had been a good year, and I was glad to get a bonus, for I was building a new home at the time. Then a new year began. All three branches of the business performed well, and we capitalized on our ideas. Changing seemed to have been a good choice. I enjoyed the new team and gained a lot of experience. Thus, it came out of the blue when, at one of our monthly management meetings at the end of the second year, it was revealed that we were operating at a loss, and results for that financial year showed a loss too.

"How can this be?" I asked. "We have significantly increased our turnover in each branch of the business."

I only received partial information and not a proper explanation, and I didn't like what I was hearing. I requested an analysis of all the different branches of the business for the next meeting, to be able to comprehend what had happened and to find out what course of action to take. The analysis was never made, and we didn't find anything out—or at least I never did. I didn't quite understand what was actually happening. The others had been together for ten years, they knew their field, and the company had been working fine during previous years. I asked around, talked to the accountant, to the managers of the other branches of the business, but I could still only get partial information.

Although I didn't yet possess my economics degree at the time, I knew something wasn't right. It was as if they were keeping something secret. But I banished the thought—why would they be hiding anything from me? I didn't understand what was going on, and the atmosphere at work started to get tense.

December slowly rolled on, and I was sadly thinking that I could say good-bye to my annual premium, even though I'd managed to put through the plans in my field and the revenue was substantial. I thought if we could follow events more carefully from the beginning of the year, we would break even. Then came the annual end-of-year meeting in December, which turned out to be rather bizarre. Perhaps as a result of my asking around, talking to my colleagues, and being "difficult," the truth came out. My intuition was right. There was a heated atmosphere at the meeting. The managing director's slip of the tongue about product guarantees gave it all away. He said, "It wasn't us who received the guarantee fee for the products marketed by us; the actual producer gave it to someone else."

"Someone else? But we are the distributors. What if something becomes faulty? No wonder we are showing a loss," said I.

Then everything came to light nice and slowly: the other managers and proprietors had formed an acquisition partnership, and that's where the profit had ended up! "There is a reason for this, and you'll soon be part of it," they said.

The world had turned upside down. I never really saw my colleagues after work since I was commuting from about hundred kilometers away. Being a new workforce gossip didn't suit me, and I never thought that this could happen. Now I realized why the service manager, with whom I had a good relationship, had asked me a few weeks before, "How come you are still around?"

I had already known at the ominous meeting that this type of business approach was not my cup of tea, and after contemplating things for a few days, I quit. It was the right decision.

I hadn't heard of Warren Buffet at the time, so I didn't know his famous saying:

> **"It takes twenty years to build a reputation and five minutes to ruin it. If you think about that, you'll do things differently."**

2.3   REMEMBER THE TITANS!

The will to win is nothing without the will to prepare.
—*Juma Ikangaa*

Let's travel back in time. We are in America in the seventies, where tension between blacks and whites is an everyday issue. They are trying to abolish racial discrimination from above, and the federal government is making resolutions relating to this. However, not everyone will take sides and will be able to identify with such strategic decision-making.

The same applies to high school students who attend a segregated institution. At this time, schools are being merged. This happens in Alexandria, Virginia, which forces two football teams to "fuse" as well. Just as in the schools, there are only white-skinned players on one of the teams and black-skinned players on the other. In this new situation, however, only one team will be selected to play in the championship. They will be the "Titans," and the leaders of the city want them to win.

The conflict is already a given, especially since they hire the fairly experienced and (with his current team) not particularly successful black coach to be head of the new, mixed team, while the white coach is only appointed to be an assistant coach. Everything relates to football in this town. The community adores their teams with a passion, yet racial differences are strong: the black and the white are equally prejudiced against each other.

The newly appointed coach—portrayed by Denzel Washington in the film *Remember the Titans*—doesn't get intimidated by the task; he sees the new, underlying possibilities instead. He asks the team members to be partners and declares that in the interests of the team, he will not tolerate any lack of respect. He makes it clear that apart from performance, nothing else matters on the field.

There are nighttime conflicts at the football camp as well as heated debates, but the coach remains consistent and adamant. By the time the football camp finishes, the team has achieved an almost totally harmonious coherence, and everyone is happy to sing the team song of the Titans.

The film offers an example—and a path to follow—for any leader; it is not solely an inspiration for those trying to find an analogy with a grand idea or a political viewpoint. You will rarely encounter a more difficult situation than the one in this film. From a professional point of view, bringing the team together, the football camp, and the championship are a very important methodological study. How to build a team and gain respect by consistent demands? How to make a fair evaluation just by looking at results? What instruments might be used to unearth the conflicts within a team?

As managers, we mustn't only concentrate on results—we also have to take into consideration the feelings and reactions of the people behind the figures, otherwise the expected result will not hold or we will not achieve any result whatsoever. A good manager uses the solutions and ways of operating of the coach in the film—criticizing, complimenting, often motivating, and sometimes, if necessary, even threatening. The manager will do this at the right time, in the right place, using whatever the situation requires. This is also how we can lead our own Titans to victory.

Every manager dreams of an effective and well-performing team. That is why it is useful to gain all the experience needed for team developing and building. Still, the most difficult challenge is rebuilding a team, and such a situation can occur at any time in a business environment. That is when help comes in handy—and when *Remember the Titans* comes to mind.

Our accomplishments are nowadays judged by teamwork rather than individual performance. The manager's key task is therefore developing and building the team. It can be carried out as illustrated in the following story.

John was given a new task. His superiors had clearly explained to him that by the end of the year they wanted a profit, and within three years they would have to reach the industrial average. Tendencies hadn't been satisfying for some time, sales turnover had stagnated, good results were on the decline, and the team was in despair. There was a lot of activity and expense, but minimal results.

After becoming acquainted with his task, John started to draw up a business and an action plan. He wanted to know each and every little detail. It is good to know the answers to the following questions if we want to reform something: Who does what, when, and how? Why, for how much, and with what result? Then comes the difficult question: evolution or revolution, that is, develop or rebuild right from the beginning?

For John, the situation shortly brought an answer. The manager of the old team and leaders from three other substantial fields left the company for various reasons. This meant that there was a possibility of revolution, since new people were being appointed into new positions. A new business plan, new tasks, a new organization, new responsibilities—all were quickly adapted to the new situation.

John, however, made a tactical error: shortly after the four leaders had left, he presented his ideas to all the team members. He figured that if he integrated them into things, they would feel more like part of the plan and identify with the objectives much more easily. In that special situation, however, what registered was that they would have to work more hours while their wages and benefits were reduced. *Aha! Now I understand why the four of them left—they must have already seen the new plan!* thought several of them, and *What does he want here? We've been absolutely fine up till now; what's all this nonsense about?* Thoughts are normally followed by actions, and before long, some of the people John might've counted upon also decided to leave the organization.

John knew the objectives that had been set by the owners. These were not to change—neither the expected result nor the deadline—whatever might happen. He was the one who had to find a solution, so he acted swiftly, adapting to the new situation. He appointed new heads from among the well-connected team members, persons with good organizational skills and strong personalities. And he planned to fill positions in a new business field via external recruitment.

He held a preliminary meeting with this new group of managers, and initially only with them. They separated the business objectives and expectations into fields. Finalizing the development of these new fields was the task of the new managers. The process was working.

The next few months were full of hard and long working days, sometimes lasting well into the night—and there was a little tension, along with successes and failures. A few people gave up and left the company, but by the end of the year there were successes to show. Those who survived the training camp—as had the members of the newly integrated football team in the film *Remember the Titans*—were not afraid anymore; they weren't hesitant because they'd had a taste of mutual success. They knew that results would follow in the years to come.

John had gained a lot of new experiences and, of course, was proud of what the new team had achieved; but above all, he was happy about what one of the team members casually told him at dinner once, after a presentation of results for the following quarter: "You were right, boss, but I admit I didn't have much faith in you at the beginning."

Productive work is a result of teamwork, yet the catalyst in any success is the leader. Team members have to be well selected, and the right person must be placed in the right position. The manager has to set intelligent objectives, develop functioning programs, and inspire a motivated organization that will take the company closer to success step by step, day after day. And of course, we have to believe that we can do it.

If you know what and how, it only depends on your perseverance regarding when you are going to achieve your objective.

2.4 ALL OR NOTHING

Do not fall into the error of the artisan who boasts of twenty years' experience in the trade whilst, in fact, he has had only one year of experience—twenty times.
—*Rodney William Whitaker, a.k.a. Trevanian*

A new boss arrives at a company. He looks around to see how the work is going. He spots a young man sitting around looking bored and immediately blows his top:

"How much is your monthly salary, son?"

"About $1,000," he answers.

"Here's $1,000! Take it and leave. I never want to see you again, you lazy bum!" The man takes the money and disappears without saying a word. An employee appears with some money in his hand and looks around helplessly.

"Have you seen the pizza guy, boss?"

Do you know this joke? Perhaps you do, perhaps you don't. You will certainly know this saying: every joke is a new joke if you've never heard it before. A manager can't make the same mistake and behave as if he is experiencing something for the first time.

Several times have I met newly appointed managers who followed their own instincts and ideas instead of first getting to know the employees and procedures, mapping out the knowledge existing within the organization, and getting information about tried and tested methods. This is one way of becoming successful, but it's not an efficient method; it requires a lot more energy than the clever solution. Furthermore, if the manager does not map out company operations and find out what traditions have been built upon first, he or she might try to implement ideas that have indeed failed before. This may demotivate employees over time, as this déjà vu feeling could make their tasks seem pointless, and they might only be carrying them out to please the boss.

A new marketing manager had been appointed. Jean-Pierre had already worked abroad; he'd gained experience in South America, and, of course, he had gotten to know the business processes existing in his homeland, France. After one short week, he asked to see his boss. "Here are my suggestions," he said, and a slide show started to roll on the projector. There wasn't a single area he didn't want to reform.

"There is nothing worth keeping, in your opinion? Will you have the time to make all the changes you would like to embark upon? And what results do you think the changes might bring?" asked his boss.

Jean-Pierre replied confidently, "This is how it works everywhere else, and it's good. It will work here too! There will be some results in a month."

"All right. See you in a month."

Time, as usual, flew by rapidly. One month passed. At their monthly meeting, Jean-Pierre demonstrated the amount of progress in the changes he had started to implement. One small task completed, others half done. This wouldn't have been a problem if our friend Jean-Pierre hadn't suspended most operational procedures so that the new decisions could have the newly laid-out rules as their basis. He didn't realize that informing the administrator straight away is very important in many situations. If there are no decision-making principles because the old ones are no longer operational and the new ones have not yet been introduced, no decisions can be made—or if we *do* manage to make a decision, it will be nowhere near what we had intended (except if the administrator is so competent that he or she senses what the right decision should be or can read our minds). You can't allow business partners to wait in today's supply market, because they might stop trusting you. In consequence, instead of improving results, business stagnated or in some areas began declining.

Jean-Pierre soon realized this and reported again shortly after the second evaluation meeting, "Boss, I have thought things over. I can now see through and comprehend the processes a lot better, and I would like to revise my original ideas." With the new suggestion, only a few processes were amended in their entirety, while most only needed modification. This only took two months, and by the end of the year their improving competitiveness was already measurable.

In a new position or workplace, it is advisable to make inquiries first. It's worth asking, asking, and asking again until the picture is complete. As Winston Churchill said, "The further backward you look, the further forward you can see." You can find out everything about ways of operating; employees' abilities and skills and their experiences; and information that is not included in the regulations but is fundamental to the operation. A new leader doesn't necessarily have to be a genius. He or she has to think globally, only utilize what actually does work, and find the best way to success. A manager can only become a credible leader if he or she tailors knowledge and experiences to a given company or position, which means taking local circumstances under consideration.

Sometimes you have to rebuild everything, but often, a fresh thought is enough. You have to decide which one is more effective.

2.5   TO WHOM ARE THEY GOING TO WAVE THE CHECKERED FLAG?

It doesn't matter who is in a winning position now or
who has been at the top. What matters is who is going
to have won after the last race has been run.
—Kimi Raikkönen

Business competition and performance are much like the world of Formula 1 racing. Seemingly only one indicator is important: obtaining the title. Yet you need to collect points for this. A race ranking is essential, and you don't need to have won every race to be able to stand on the highest level of the podium at the end of the season. Winning a race is a noteworthy result, but it is only one stage in a long series of events. And it isn't easy to achieve this result. It's a result of teamwork, not just personal performance.

It certainly matters how the group of mechanics of a Formula 1 team is made up, and whether procedures are well prepared and planned out. Professional and effective methods and techniques are needed. Well-designed aerodynamic elements and quality tires are important building blocks on the path to success. Beating a previous record for a tire-change pit stop may be decisive in the race and so aid victory. It also makes a difference how well the driver has examined the given racecourse before the race and how competent he is. This is a complex, multifactor system, the individual elements of which need to function and fit into each other perfectly in order to get the best possible results.

The performance of an enterprise is also a result of taking lots of little steps. Sales turnover and results are two factors that we have to take into consideration when evaluating and ranking an economic enterprise. These will decide who stays at the top and who lags behind in business competition. It is impossible to stay at the top for a long period of time if the minute details of the operation have not been adequately planned and organized, or if precise measuring points and information that can predict approaching or existing problems in time are not in place. We will end up lagging behind if we only concentrate on the final result, do not notice performance losses in time, and only interfere in procedures when it is already too late.

Certain events we might never think of can often influence results too. A manager should always consider everything that is or might be important. There is a reason many organizations use the Balanced Scorecard model. The book *Strategy Maps: Converting Intangible Assets into Tangible Outcomes* by Robert S. Kaplan and David P. Norton provides several examples of how to map a company's value-added processes and how to measure performance in a complex way. You will be able to build a balanced scorecard by using this approach, starting with strategic objectives.

Customer-satisfaction-checking measures, internal procedures, and learning and development factors are normally to be added to financial indicators. These are the tokens of future performance. You can then identify sub-objectives so that you get a comprehensive and accurate picture of the effectiveness of subprocesses via observing customer expectations, internal procedures, and the developmental prospects involved. A static evaluation of financial indicators must therefore be supplemented by a measurement of trends. Applying these might, in the long run, guarantee a better chance of our enterprise winning a podium position over and over again.

In the midnineties, a medium-sized privately owned organization started up. Its leaders wanted to expand their already existing branch of an office-technology business. Information technology (IT) was booming at the time. Commodore 64, the hit of the eighties, was already being superseded by the XT and faster versions; PCs had also appeared. In 1949, John von Neumann declared that "information technology has reached the boundaries of its development." In 1990, the management of our organization was sure that this was wrong as a forecast; this was only the tip of the iceberg, or just the beginning of things, and IT would create an abundance of business opportunities. Based on the saying "A new business needs a new manager," I was given the job of setting up the IT business line. I threw myself into it, albeit with little experience. Nonetheless, I knew at the time that performance could only be controlled and developed with measurable progress.

I started to plan what and how we could achieve, see what resources were available, and figure out how we were going to measure all of it. Two months passed, and I was approaching the final stages of preparing my business plan and creating an organization of ten members. The manager of the codivision observed my activities with a grin on his face. "Look," he said one morning, in a friendly manner, "what's all this planning and calculation for? Come with me, I'll introduce you to the chairman of the cooperative, and you can sell him a Commodore. You can't expect to get anywhere near photocopier and typewriter sales, of course, but you can make a decent turnover." So the encouragement was there. I had doubts whether the business was going to take off.

What's all this planning for? Let's jump right in! I carried on, for "it's only worth working with precision ..." Fortunately, the next piece of "friendly advice" only blew the fuse when our first order came in: "I know, I can see that the business is not taking off, so I've got some secondhand telephones you can certainly sell for a good price." I politely refused his offer, saying I couldn't possibly deprive him of such a phenomenal business opportunity.

That's when I thought that I would overtake him or my knowledge was worth nothing. Yet I hesitated. I might easily fail. I didn't have time to wait for the energy invested to fully recoup. Market research, organizing on the basis of customer needs, application of an accurate measuring scheme in order to be able to always control everything—it all seemed like a waste of time. Was it possible that we had lost out? Would it not have been enough to implement the management technique of the office automation division?

No, life has proved that it wouldn't have. After initial stumbles made in the first year despite an adequately chosen strategy and personnel and also with some well-planned processes, over a few months our turnover took off—and by the end of the year, it had greatly overtaken that of the office automation division. We got to know the market, the possibilities, and the risks—and the system began to function.

An appropriate combination of manager, team, and processes can help you take the lead in any competition. It is of course questionable whether the manager is capable of seeing all the risks and realizing all the opportunities, and whether he or she can make the most of a given situation. Several different measures are therefore important for victory to be gained in business. They will also indicate where to amend and improve, where to make progress and develop, which field needs more attention than usual, and where to interfere if there is a problem. The world of business is more complicated than a car-racing track, though, because there everything is about the race and even if they do several tire changes and refuelings, at the annual meeting the key indicators still have to tally.

The whole process is made up of subprocesses, so you have to keep your eyes peeled.

2.6 LONG LIVE THE MIXED TEAMS!

*You can always learn something new from a
quick and competitive teammate.*
—*Felipe Massa*

When dealing with everyday problems, the age and gender of team members make no difference. What matters is that their knowledge, skills, and abilities complement each other. I myself believe that well-functioning mixed teams can achieve outstanding results. Concerning some special tasks, restrictive factors can of course hinder team members, but as we know, the exception proves the rule.

In my opinion, mixed teams are usually more successful simply because they are built on a healthy combination of tradition and innovation. Based on experiences gained and actual expectations, tradition opens the way to successful operations. In a good sense, it doesn't mean lacking change but, instead, slow steps, a slower but surer progress, so that innovation is still present. Innovation either means revolutionary ideas or smaller creations, yet an ability to break out of or move beyond the routine.

Imagine a work team of young people with fresh knowledge. In theory, they know everything. However, since they haven't got any experience, they can't apply the theories effectively. They are innovators, but they lack experience for efficient implementation. Now imagine a more mature and experienced group of professionals. They are wise, they have experience, but their fresh and risk-taking attitude is a thing of the past, so their interest in trying new, innovative ideas might be inhibited by routine and good practice.

Age, to a certain extent, defines our method of thinking. Chapter 22 in *Is That Me?* by Mark Miers looks at what brain research tells us about ourselves. According to research, wisdom comes with age, and this process can be measured. As we reach the age of twenty-five, our brain starts to shrink, and by the time we reach ninety, it has lost 10 to 15 percent of its weight. It comes as no surprise then that fewer scientific discoveries are made by people over thirty and that for those over forty or fifty, there is a good chance of underachieving in memory games when playing against younger people.

As a direct result, this means that the more our brain shrinks, the more serious our mental deterioration becomes. Yet research has proved that the brain mainly shrinks because of superfluous cells and a loss of water, while it is continuously (re)shaping itself. Until the age of fifty, the myelin sheath that covers the neurons and within which stimuli travel is constantly thickening. That's why people in their fifties can combine information more easily and make more thoughtful decisions than those in their thirties. The secret lies in more life experience and better utilization of this. No wonder young people take unnecessary risks—they are revolutionaries who are banging their heads against a wall without thinking as events unfold. Older persons are more mature, though at times they won't take a risk even if it's worth it.

In my opinion, there are a variety of reasons for making more mature decisions. We make decisions based upon our values, our acquired theoretical knowledge, and our skills. Supposing that values are the same, there is still a basic difference between the older and younger generations: the experience gained. This, through making use of our acquired theoretical knowledge, helps us to be more effective and more fruitful in our jobs. You can gain experience in three different ways: garnering professional experience through work, gathering experience from senior colleagues, or gleaning experience with the help of reference books and training programs.

The old and young jointly combine theory and practice—in other words, knowledge and innovation. They create a synergy of different elements and factors that brings about better performance and results than if all were merely added up or just coordinated. This is where the advantage and strength of mixed working teams lies.

When tradition and innovation combine, efficiency increases.

2.7   GET TO KNOW BUSINESS PROCESSES

*Efficiency is doing things right; effectiveness
is doing the right things.*
—*Peter Drucker*

Thomas's company had bought a smaller enterprise and its brand as an addition to its product portfolio. The enterprise's profile was that of barcode technology, which opened a gate to a specialized field. The acquiring company, according to its product portfolio, had been known and acknowledged on the market for years for supplying computer networks. It had been present in each and every marketing channel where these products were being sold. With the new product range, however, they were entering the world of specialists.

The products of the enterprise purchased were mostly sold to contractors dealing with the implementation of barcode technology in specific projects. Thomas, as the marketing and commercial manager of the company, thought that the acquisition would bring about quick, new opportunities for the existing products of the company too and that their turnover would not simply show an aggregate but might be a little more. So they didn't do much planning and started to offer their own product portfolio to the partners of the newly acquired enterprise; they also began to sell the special products through their own business channels.

They threw themselves in too hastily and wanted to achieve results too fast. They didn't take into consideration that although the two business models overlapped in some respects, they could not be aggregated without making some changes. They would have had to make more accurate surveys and explore the circle of partners to be able to understand by whom, why, and when the products of the acquired enterprise would be bought. The situation with things after the acquisition did not exactly help new product sales to the new partners. Mixing the two markets so swiftly and recklessly, Thomas and his colleagues were like bulls in a china shop. Everything was destroyed—business connections, profit, as well as a good relationship with the specialists.

There had to be a complete reconsideration of the future of the product and selling operations, for the sales of the previously successful brand had seen a significant decline. A quote by Albert Szent-Györgyi came to Thomas's mind: "Research is to see what everybody else has seen, and to think what nobody else has thought." Had Thomas made wiser decisions, he could've been an explorer, though this way he only gained some unpleasant experiences. In my opinion, you can learn just as much from the worst practice as the best practice.

Occasionally, before making a marketing decision, it's worth opening the book *Marketing Management* by Philip Kotler and Kevin Lane Keller for almost a thousand pages of method, description, classification, and example. In this case, Thomas should have investigated both the existing and new business processes. You can only choose the right strategy once similarities and differences between them have been established. A mutual market appearance might have to wait, and we will only experience the results of any synergy at a later stage, though there certainly won't be any falling back or negative experiences. Thomas knew he had to keep this experience in mind. If two enterprises are successful separately, it doesn't mean that, together, their performance will attain an aggregate. It may be more, or it may be less.

This story reminds me of how my university physics professor drew our attention to the restricted use of the reversibility principle: "If we rub two objects against each other, they will heat up, but this doesn't mean that if two objects heat up, they will start rubbing against each other." I advise everyone before starting a similar project to first think, ask, and analyze the situation—and then think again to see whether things need changing and, if so, in what order.

I hope nobody will come to the decision—based on the proverb "A bird in the hand is worth two in the bush"—that it's not worth developing or buying a firm. You have to be sensible. We need *both* birds, but instead of straight away, we might only acquire them the day after tomorrow.

> **Don't be mean about spending time on understanding business processes; you might only achieve the desired result at a later stage, but you will achieve it.**

2.8   WINNING STRATEGIES

> *Change or die.*
> —*Jack Welch*

It is hard to come up with a lasting, winning strategy in today's economic environment, which is most of all dominated by dynamic changes. Globalization means widening competition. Increasing technological development creates new ways of operating, and new habits and requirements. All this is happening at an ever-accelerating pace. Generational customer differences have always existed, yet the changes mentioned before have speeded these up.

As we prepared for the exit exam from secondary school thirty years ago, only one colleague of mine had a PC; it was mostly a status symbol at the time and not a device aiding enumeration and counting. It is now a cheap, almost valueless object. The PC revolution started in the nineties. Within a short period of twenty years, the capacity of the first PCs were multiplied and squeezed into much smaller portable laptops. For persons familiar with them, there is now a multitude of software to aid faster and more effective work. Twentysomethings who have grown up on computer games and the Internet are naturally much better at handling computers than those in their forties and fifties, who only learned how to use them as adults.

We cannot form a company strategy on time if we don't understand the ongoing business processes and trends. As everything changes— and changes rapidly—the first step should always be collection of data. "The time spent on exploration is seldom considered to be a waste," said Sun Tzu, the Chinese military general. This is especially relevant in today's economic climate, when, because of great changes, previously successful business practices might have become outdated by tomorrow. To be able to stay prosperous in a changing business environment, an enterprise often has to alter its old-fashioned ways of doing things. It is advisable to concentrate on the principal activity of the enterprise, because a large amount of information has to be processed within a short period of time, using limited resources.

It is recommended that anything that is not part of this activity be outsourced to enterprises that deal with such issues. You can be even more efficient if you find business allies—partners that you share common business interests with. You can develop more swiftly and have a chance to overtake your competitors by marketing new ideas and products, which may then enable you to create a temporary monopoly situation. This is only if the products have been made by observing customer needs and prospective trends, taking what market competitors are doing and producing into consideration and introducing them before others. This is how you stay a step ahead of your rivals.

In his 1999 book *Kotler on Marketing: How to Create, Win, and Dominate Markets*, Philip Kotler writes that it is the result of the ever-accelerating changes that a twelve-year-old girl says about her nine-year-old sister, "She is a different generation!" The younger sister listens to different music, plays different video games, and adores different movie stars and heroes. These changes are detectable if you spend enough time on market research and analysis. According to Kotler, only those companies in the twenty-first century that use modern, up-to-date tactics as opposed to sticking to old-fashioned ways and methods will remain successful. Kotler cites certain business tactics as old-fashioned and up-to-date, and I'll quote a few of them here:

Old	Modern
Produce everything within the company.	Subcontract as much as possible.
Make developments based on your own products.	Make developments based on the products of your strongest competitor.
Advance alone.	Cooperate with business partners.
Work with functional divisions.	Work with multidisciplinary groups.
Concentrate on local matters.	Observe both local and global matters.
Be product-centered.	Be market- and product-centered.
Do slow product development.	Do fast product development.

But methods and trends can change and for sure will change in time, as the environment is constantly changing. In 2006, in the 12th edition of *Marketing Management*, Philip Kotler and Kevin Lane Keller give a most precise definition of marketing excellence of best practices:

Poor	Good	Excellent
product driven	market driven	market driving
mass-market oriented		niche oriented and
	segment oriented	customer oriented
	augmented	customer solutions
product offer	product offer	offer

average product quality	better than average	legendary
average service quality	better than average	legendary
end-product oriented	core-product oriented	core-competency oriented
function oriented	process oriented	outcome oriented
reacting to competitors	benchmarking competitors	leapfrogging competitors
supplier exploitation	supplier preference	supplier partnership
dealer exploitation	dealer support	dealer partnership
price driven	quality driven	value driven
average speed	better than average	legendary
hierarchy	network	teamwork
vertically integrated	flattened organization	strategic alliances
stockholder driven	stakeholder driven	societally driven

When we make a comparison with these classifications, we can see how modern and how effective the marketing tactics of enterprises are. Nevertheless, methods are only tools, and since enterprises are run by people, a certain tool might not be equally successful in every eventuality. You have to find the most suitable method for your own team.

We all do things well in different ways. Perhaps a better example for this is the Bud Spencer and Terence Hill duo. Bud, a.k.a. Carlo Pedersoli, is the childishly naive and somewhat carefree guy, and Terence, a.k.a. Mario Girotti, is the meticulous and dutiful actor. Even though the 1967 film *God Forgives, I Don't* (also known as *No Mercy*) wasn't the first one they had acted in together, it was the one to bring them fame and success. This was followed by numerous other joint films in which they mainly dealt with dangerous situations together but made use of their own personal techniques for dealing with them. The chapter related to this time period in Bud Spencer's biography begins with the following two quotes: "It matters not how slow you go as long as you do not stop" (Confucius) and "It is possible that everything is true. It is true that everything is possible." (Bud Spencer).

In my opinion, the first quote is about persistence. What the second one tells me, however, is that with perseverance you can achieve almost anything but, of course, only if you apply a suitable method. Bud and Terence Hill possessed suitable methods, and even though they used different slapping techniques, they always won.

For a winning strategy, this method begins with effective knowledge of the market. A company has to gather all the information needed to be able to specify the most suitable strategies and tactics to follow, all on a regular basis. This is an oft-repeated task, and a decision is made according to the information gained; then the implementation process begins. Even if nothing else changes—which we know is nowhere near likely to be true—a new situation will still arise on the market. We can expect some reaction from our rivals in reference to our actions, so we have to keep a check on implementation as well as launching the whole process, with updated data, again and again.

According to Philip Kotler, the action scheme recognized by marketing experts consists of five main steps, which are:

$$R \rightarrow STP \rightarrow MM \rightarrow I \rightarrow C$$

where

- R (research) = market research,
- STP (segmentation, targeting, positioning) = levels of marketing strategy,
- MM = marketing mix, the level marketing tactic also known as 4P (product, price, place, promotion),
- I = implementation, and
- C = control, feedback, and an evaluation of results.

We can find many similarities here with the Deming PDCA cycle: plan, do, check, and act. I personally think that feedback is vital so that we can bring our business strategy and tactics up to date if necessary. We can, however, judge our situation incorrectly, or an unforeseen and sudden market or an internal requirement system change may arise. As Ted Levitt said, "A product is not a product unless it sells. Otherwise it is merely a museum piece." It wouldn't be appropriate to fill our warehouse with such products.

Famax Ltd. was a subcontractor of a company making electronic products. They produced switching units for vacuum cleaners and washing machines. The monthly demand was inconsistent, but the annual average amount had been fairly steady for years. They optimized their production range in order to maximize output. As a result, they managed to cut down their production expenses significantly, although the value of the fittings that were not made to order—and were stored onsite—saw a notable increase. Since orders did come in sooner or later, it was still worth producing goods this way in spite of the additional cost of stock-financing for several months. Feedback—monitoring what kind of market forecasts were available to a customer and what sort of developments they were considering—was omitted from the process. Famax Ltd. was therefore startled when its customer announced at the end of the year their wish to change the product. The company could have avoided the stock accumulated over several months becoming "museum objects" had it carefully observed every part of the business process.

It is not enough to merely know the method—you have to give attention to careful implementation too.

2.9   GET THE MIRRORS OUT!

A mirror that you hold in front of others
should be double-sided.
—Daniel Seeberger

If making a decision involves many uncertainties, we become insecure. We might feel as if we are walking around in a roomful of mirrors in an enchanted castle, and we perceive ourselves and reality differently in each and every mirror. It is fundamental when making a decision that we look in the appropriate mirror—one that does not distort our image and shows us a realistic picture of ourselves. This is the only way to realistically gauge what we are able or unable to do, what is and what might not be achievable. This is also important to establish and estimate if we wish to make the right decision, what risks and traps we will have to avoid, and what facilities are available to gain a victory.

We know of several different types of mirrors. We have to choose well so that we get the right support in a given situation for making an appropriate decision. A flat mirror is excellent—it gives an undistorted, objective picture of the situation and the facts. It nevertheless also occurs that we may need to examine a problem's surroundings or environment, and to facilitate this, we need to magnify it so that we can see all the little details. For that, we need to take a concave mirror out, which will act as a magnifying glass. It might also occur that our fears become oversized so that we overreact to some pieces of information and give them much more attention than necessary. That's when we need to look for a convex mirror that will make a problem appear smaller; and this will help us realize that we have overstated things and placed too much emphasis on them, so that we saw a lion instead of a mouse.

Once upon a time, there was a team all the managers feared—a group of tough guys. When I became their manager, some of my colleagues gloated about this with a grin on their faces. "Good luck," they said, though they didn't believe in it.

The first year passed quite peacefully, but at its end my team members wanted to discuss their earnings. "Expectations are high, but the salary is low," they said, adding that I shouldn't expect quality work given this situation. As we know, everyone likes looking at his own salary in a concave mirror. There's nothing wrong with this if, from time to time, we can put things right. If we have really overreacted, we can rest assured that we can at least come to a conclusion based on realistic information. I had to mirror the guys' expectations with reality so that they would be able to see the truth themselves—truth being something they believe and are not just told about.

In difficult conditions, it always pays to take the straight and narrow path. We started the new year with a meeting that everyone was invited to, not only the managers. It was hard to enter the room or to take the first step, but I did it. I told them what our expectations were and also the reasons behind them. They were nodding; they accepted the analysis. Then came the difficult bit, telling them how much we were paying and how much they could get elsewhere. I explained how others did it and how expectations, conditions, and salaries differed from place to place, emphasizing what we did better and what others could be criticized for. We didn't need a distorting mirror, only a concave and a convex one so that the differences became embedded in people's minds. They got the point, and I was reassured by their firm handshakes when they said good-bye. The mirror game was successful; I led the team for four years without much tension or any significant problems. To achieve such success, we ourselves also have to look in the appropriate mirror.

Some of us don't like looking in the mirror when we get up in the morning. And it is even more difficult to look into our personal, internal mirror, as using such a mirror requires better self-knowledge and situational awareness. Those who succeed here will be able to appropriately prepare in regard to each correct decision and support it with adequate information.

> **The mirror shows you what to look out for. The challenge is to find the most suitable one.**

2.10 THE ANALOGY OF LIFE AND COFFEE

The client is our best friend. We don't deceive them,
we pay attention to them and help them.
—Doug Larson

In formerly socialist countries like Hungary, the real importance of marketing only began after a change of regime. The political changes affected the economy, the changing economy affected society, the changing society influenced consumption, and consumption had an impact back on the economy. Starting in the early nineties, this cycle put changes swiftly into motion but, unfortunately, also had a lot of negative consequences. Between Hungary and Austria, the iron curtain left only a limited place for business exchange and tourism. When the borders opened up after the regime transition, we got a green light to the West, which started with "fridge-buying tourism" to Vienna and carried on with the conception that "what's foreign is better."

Thousands of Hungarian tourists went to purchase refrigerators and other things in Wien malls, where the presentation was more appealing. In the socialist market conception, product and service competition were not supported, so manufacturers didn't pay attention to marketing, packaging, and design. That doesn't mean these were always bad-quality products, but for sure the marketing and design were not attractive. In ten years of market development, this misconception—which was a result of deficit management and the appealing packaging of foreign goods—is now slowly becoming a part of the past. The moral of this story is that packaging is marketing. It is part of a company's tempting us to consume. It is the actual product that is important to us, yet we often give in to temptation and buy something purely because of its packaging.

How much should we resist temptation? Here comes another story. Once upon a time, a group of former students, all fairly successful at work, got together to visit their old professor. What started as a pleasant conversation soon became a series of complaints about the stress they were experiencing at work and in life. The host offered some coffee to his guests and soon returned from the kitchen with a large coffeepot and several different cups—porcelain, plastic, glass, and even crystal ones among them. Some of the cups were cheap while others were more expensive, and there were some real curiosities too.

"Take one from the tray," said the professor. When each cup had been taken, the professor looked around and said the following: "Have you noticed that all the expensive cups have been taken but the simpler or, God forbid, chipped ones have not? I must say that it is only natural that you all want the best for yourselves, but this is exactly where all your stress and anxiety lies. What you originally wanted was a coffee, and not the cups, but you selected the fanciest ones and secretly even carefully observed your friends' cups too. Look, your life is the coffee, and the cups are work, money, and social status. They are the means to sustain and contain life, but they won't change its original quality. It often happens that while we concentrate on the cup, we forget to enjoy the God-given coffee. Don't let the cups mislead you! Enjoy the coffee instead!"

What lesson might you draw from this? Only that you mustn't fall for the slickest marketing or shiniest packaging because they are often simply trying to make you take a look at or buy a product. You should believe in marketing that has already been proven and is not a mere promise.

If you happen to sit on the other side of the desk, as a manager, you should see how you might be able to increase revenue. In my opinion, it is only ethical to advertise your company's real values. We have a good chance of our customers returning to us again and again if we don't ever deceive them, because they will trust us.

Trust and trustworthiness have client-keeping properties in a business race.

2.11 LIFE AFTER THE MONOPOLY SITUATION

Successful business enterprises deal in special products,
presented by an impressive story. It's much more profitable
than do as others but a touch better.
—Seth Godin

You can take a great leap ahead if you manage to create a monopoly situation with a product or service, even if only for a transitional period. Even though there had been similar initiations before, *Szuperinfó*, which is now distributed nationwide, was the first free advertisement newspaper to be released in Hungary. Upon its release, the free paper was considered a novelty; the advertisers paid, and it skimmed off the market. The first such free, informational weekly paper was published in Eger in 1990. In two years it had become the largest-selling paper and, because of its innovative nature, the choice of weekend reading for domestic households.

You should note that this is just one year after the change of regime, when all advertising was interesting reading. A demand market was transforming itself into a supply market. The paper was launched at the right time. As soon as the distributors popped them into mailboxes, the whole family started going through them, browsing through the news and especially the advertisements. These were important and useful pieces of information in an expanding market.

Twenty years have since passed, and we can see a growing number of notes on mailboxes saying "No advertising or flyers." Roadsides are covered with billboards, and the media is trying to make the best use of the twelve minutes per hour advertising time on commercial TV channels. Ads come at us from left, right, and center, for we have also become a consumer society. Advertisements have become so numerous that they have lost their original value. We have had enough of them! Even *Szuperinfó* has lost its monopoly position, although it has kept up its position as the widest-distribution free paper in Hungary during this past couple of decades. It paid off to have started at the right time and to have been in the right position. The initial monopoly situation helped maximize profit. This should be seen as a good base and resource for developments, as we mustn't stop.

The question is whether a manufacturer or service provider is capable of changing and of making changes in time according to what market dictates arise in connection with each commodity or service that enjoys a monopoly situation, especially as the profit rate of being in a monopoly position attracts competition. Whether the monopoly is able to get itself prepared and form a new strategy in time for the appearance of competitors is also an issue, as is whether it is able to stay good, interesting, useful, and cheap enough for customers in order to keep some of its acquired and beneficial market position. The appearance and increasing number of competitors can bring about a murderous price war that may reach profit-destroying levels. Cutting down on expenses might be an opener, but it is even more effective to search for new ways of doing things, for innovation.

Fornetti Ltd. was facing the same issues when it was established as a family business in 1997, producing frozen food in a converted detached house in Kecskemét. The company sold its products in Hungary through a then-unknown network of exhibition bakeries—where customers could watch their bread, pastry, and other goods being baked right in front of their eyes—and within a franchise system. On their way to work, people were happy to munch away on savory scones outside shops while they waited for their means of public transportation. The company built its great popularity and publicity in a short period of time with this opportunity and with this idea. Still, a question remained whether the enterprise was capable of keeping its market-leading position, especially as, in the meantime, other minor and more serious competitors had begun to spring up, among them multinational chains.

Fornetti stood its ground so well that in 1999, the Fornetti franchise made its way across Hungarian borders—initially only to the country's neighbors, but today it is present in more than twenty other countries. The owner of the firm rather instructively said in one of his statements, "I know it very well that customers will not pay for yesterday's success tomorrow. To keep their confidence, you always have to provide newer, more, and better."

The success recipe for keeping customers is always providing newer, better, and something different.

2.12 GOOD TACTICS AT THE RIGHT TIME

Whoever wins the game might not have necessarily played well. He/she can only be certain that he/she has avoided making a vital mistake, which the opponent could have taken advantage of.
—Temesi Ferenc

We were preparing for a merger with another company and, according to the plans, this process was to be brought about in three years. It might have been justifiable to allow a longer period of time to make a successful transition, since there were heaps of tasks to undertake. There may be several acquisitional objectives during company mergers, such as market share, assets, and the possible synergies of the association; yet the purchaser also takes on these responsibilities and, with them, the company's business risks. To reduce the risks arising from purchasing a business and also because of price negotiations, the buyer must request a thorough, legal, financial, and taxation-related screening. If everything proves to be satisfactory, the second step can be taken: reorganizing business procedures.

The objective, naturally, is to increase market share, relying on forming synergies and optimizing the operative activities (development, production, logistics). However, the transformation in regard to the product and service quality of the firm has to remain invisible to other business partners. In our case, the merger had already been made public, and we were only waiting for final authorization. So we started making moves on internal reorganization as if the merger had already happened. Mutual objectives were established, and everything was realizable, though only on paper. Groups, in which both parties represented themselves, formed in every region, and they started to lay down the regional objectives on the basis of the central business and operating goals. An exchange of detailed information was, of course, necessary for this. Both parties got to know each other's business ideas, plans, and operational procedures as well as plans and timing related to the introduction of new commodities.

We had been doing the preparation work for approximately a year and a half and observed the unfolding events rather uneasily. The results and target values set for the three-year period didn't change, yet we only had a year and a half for the implementation procedure. "Can we do it in such a short time?" we asked ourselves. The tension intensified, and then the long preparation and waiting finally ended when the Brussels Commission authorizing European mergers decided that the acquisition could not be made. All our plans became worthless! After a year and a half, life carried on as before, and we became market competitors once again.

It is impossible to make up for lost time, but everything became very urgent. Everything should have been done yesterday. As one stressful situation ended, another came along, and we started to get worried over the loss of our market share. We were working on the introduction and launching of a new product for the following year. We wanted to fill a market niche and were expecting a serious business result. This planned development had been suspended because of the merger plans, and our competitor was also aware of this. Since the introductory deadline had been postponed for a year, we started planning again, though in vain. Unfortunately, our ex-merger partner, who had become our competitor again, knew this too. What we found out was that they had a product that could be marketed within a few months' time. If this were to happen, we would be too late.

We started a mad race and talked over all the possible ways of acting, wondering how we could appear on the market with the right commodity ahead of our competitor. We came to the conclusion that developing a new product was physically impossible but finding an existing one that could easily be adapted to market needs would be a workable solution. As a result of strenuous looking and intensive group work, we found a product we could market with minimal adaptation—ahead of our competitor. The plan for marketing our product and market share was based on simple logic. We intended to make our product visible and accessible everywhere with an aggressive advertising campaign and direct marketing, thus gaining a third of the available market. We could achieve a strong position and gain a leading market share in this way. The aggressive marketing campaign and the element of surprise had its desired effect: our competitor put off introducing its own product by half a year and has never managed to develop it to a threatening degree since then. First a business competitor, then a partner, then again a competitor—it was an interesting situation.

If I'd had any doubts about how important it is to choose the right tactic in business, they would have disappeared in a flash when I saw how successful this introduction was. A saying from Sun Tzu, the Chinese military general, comes to mind: the outcome of every war is decided in the last moment before the first battle. Our business battles commenced again after a year and a half of silence. We won the first battle, as we had found a way to move on even within the worst-case scenario. However, business is not a war but a competition, where you have to prove yourself over and over again. We never really got to know why our merger partner, who was downgraded as a competitor, had hesitated instead of searching for a similar way to go, but we were informed that the market position we had obtained was a sore spot for them. Being cautious had driven us to use the right tactics. We did what Sun Tzu recommended in his book *The Art of War*: "If you know the enemy and know yourself, you need not fear the result of a hundred battles. If you know yourself but not the enemy, for every victory gained you will also suffer a defeat. If you know neither the enemy nor yourself, you will succumb in every battle." In other words, do not underestimate your enemy, because that might be exactly what they are expecting.

As we have seen, business competition can generate extreme situations: partner today, competitor tomorrow. We live in an age of overproduction, oversupply, and too many ads. In a cutthroat battle for clients, we need to stop and take a breath, though, or we will run out of ammunition. We can create this break with an innovative idea or with the element of surprise.

William C. Taylor and Polly LaBarre write in their book *Mavericks at Work: Why the Most Original Minds in Business Win* that the way to stand out from the crowd is to have distinctive ideas about where one's industry should be heading. The book is not about best practices but about the practices of the future. It gives us an insight into—and lists case studies regarding—the new ways of making business plans, as well as management, competition, and success in our century. Peter Carril, coach for the Princeton Tigers for twenty-nine years, famously said, "The strong take from the weak, but the smart take from the strong." The Tigers regularly proved themselves against larger, faster, and physically stronger opponents. The authors of *Mavericks at Work* wanted to prove that this theory also applied to what was going on in the life of business, as they are successful because they are smarter and original ... acting on time!

Act smart and in time!

2.13 THE CREATIVE PENGUINS OF MADAGASCAR

> *An enterprise cannot survive today if it only*
> *repeats what it was doing yesterday.*
> *If it doesn't expand, it will die like a living being,*
> *and if it stops growing it will start agonizing.*
> —E. L. Doctorow

Alex the lion, Marty the zebra, Melman the giraffe, and Gloria the hippopotamus try to return to New York with the help of a group of penguins. The penguins have managed to fix up an old aircraft wreck with meticulous work, precision, and some rather unique, creative ways of operating. After a somewhat unusual but still creative takeoff, it soon becomes apparent that there will be trouble with the engines, for one of them stops and the other one catches fire.

The leader of the penguins makes a swift decision and announces on the loudspeaker: "Attention, this is your captain speaking. I have good and bad news. The good news is that we will soon be landing. The bad news is that we are going to crash."

The passengers shout desperately, shaking with fear. Meanwhile, the penguins are trying to find a solution to the problem at a crazy pace to avoid the crash. Then a miracle happens: they manage to open a huge parachute. The wobbling aircraft lands nice and slowly, and everybody survives. The creativity of the penguins—and, of course, the screenwriter—is unlimited; the protagonists of *Madagascar 2* all survive.

From a professional point of view, I must say: hats off to the penguin team. They all knew their tasks and didn't give up in the most hopeless situation. They were able to ask the right questions and get adequate answers—and last but not least, to find the right solution for every eventuality and situation. An admirable performance! The routine part is finding a solution to a problem, and the solution in itself reveals a myriad of possibilities for creativity and innovation. Managers, too, should take this message on board. Judging and analyzing a situation can be learned by accurately applying well-established methods. Routine alone is not always enough to find the right way to go. There is always a good drop of innovation and creativity in truly great business offerings.

The fastest and most effective answer to the question of *why* is routine, to *what* is innovation, and to *how* is an amalgamation of the two. The outcome is the same—a tactic that adapts to the situation, meaning the solution. Or as Bruce Pandolfini said, "It is wise to plan, but the best plans are flexible and they can be altered." Creativity and innovation have a determining role to play in business life. The main thing is that they should work when the company is successful but also if there is danger or a panic situation.

Bolko von Oetinger, manager of the Boston Consulting Group in Munich, and Henrich von Pierer, former managing director of Siemens, elaborate in their book *A Passion for Ideas: How Innovators Create the New and Shape Our World* on how innovation is an indispensable tool for any developing company. If you are not aware of this fact, you enter a dead end, which no company thinking in the long term can afford to do in today's swiftly changing business world. The two experts state that the tested instruments of innovative firms also comprise the following:

- new technical developments
- managing research and development
- controlling the quality of the workforce

The mere use of these instruments is not enough, however. A firm that has a good innovation policy will not necessarily become successful. According to von Oetinger and Pierer, one of the factors standing in the way of innovation is the difficulty of not being able to get rid of old habits. Continuing or previously successful results can linger on in our minds and be so strong that we become unable to use any other system or other rules that might help us prolong this success. Being successful leads to stronger beliefs and organizational self-confidence, which then make the implementing of changes harder.

Experience reveals that a firm producing a market-leading commodity that it distributes with great success freezes the given situation; it then becomes difficult to turn out something different or even to reinvent the existing product. There is no greater force holding you back from developing new items than success. A lot of companies have lost the art of forgetting, which is necessary when it comes to innovation, according to von Oetinger and Pierer. Perhaps this is why Nokia, the former market leader in mobile and telecommunications technology, has gotten into such a problematic state. Not realizing that smartphones had taken over, it didn't adjust in time and lost its position.

Success is necessary, though, to keep motivation at a high level in both managers and employees. I don't think it is a hindrance for a company to have a top-selling product or way of doing things—in fact, this can be a good base for further improvements. Business is just like a sports competition: winning a single race doesn't guarantee that one will win the next one too without making any effort. And even if I have strenuously trained to win, and have won in the past, I might not "take the cake" in the next round ... but I will still have a fair chance. To be among the first again and again could be one's aim, but you need to feel the spirit of achievement that will drive you toward new goals. A new race brings about a new situation that you will need to prepare for, sometimes making little changes, sometimes overriding all that has gone before.

Results and achievements cannot be repeated if we don't aim to make reforms.

2.14 NECESSARY RISKS

> *It's necessary to take risks, and to follow*
> *certain paths whilst abandoning others.*
> *No one is able to choose without fear.*
> —*Paulo Coelho*

Do you remember the film *Seventeen Moments of Spring*? The story takes place in the spring of 1945, during the last weeks of the Second World War in Berlin. The protagonist is Max Otto von Stirlitz SS-Standartenführer, a high-ranking officer for the German defense, who is in fact a Soviet spy, Maxim Isaev. Recalling the story, we immediately find ourselves in the middle of a spy film, full of secrets, bluffing, and gutsy action. Or perhaps you have seen *Where Eagles Dare*. The MI6 delegates a group of seven persons to rescue General George Carnaby from Schloss Adler castle, near Werfen, where he is being held captive, before the Nazis can interrogate him and get him to reveal the details of the Normandy landings.

The story of my grandfather might also be worthy of a film. During the First World War, he became a Russian prisoner of war. He was held captive for five years in faraway Siberia, a place in which countless startling and interesting events happened. Luckily, he was good at learning foreign languages, and during this extended period of time he learned to speak Russian fluently. This helped him along his way home, when he had to travel through half of Russia—which owing to the battles of the red and white guards wasn't an easy task. He didn't realize at the time that his knowledge of Russian would come in handy again a few years later.

He arrived in his birth town of Arad, which was then a part of Romania, in 1921. He fumed with indignation, thinking that it would have been much more useful to learn Romanian in Siberia. The Great Depression of the thirties destroyed my grandfather's furniture factory, and nobody expected that it could get any worse. It did—the Second World War broke out! My grandfather's factory was heavily bombed by the Americans and almost all of it was demolished. They could only rescue some of the machinery from the flames.

In 1944, when Romania took the side of the Allies, my grandfather was taken to a forced labor camp. There were Germans, Hungarians, and Slovaks in his unit. One weekend as the war was coming to an end, a Romanian officer appeared in the camp and announced that the Slovaks could go but that the rest were staying. After taking a look at the people putting their hands up, my grandfather decided to do the same, indicating that he was also a Slovak. The officer got suspicious and ordered another Slovak to talk to him. My grandfather began to talk in Russian, and the Slovak used his own mother tongue. They hardly understood one another.

The Slovak pointed at my grandpa and said, "He is not Slovakian!"

My grandfather looked startled and said to the officer, "He is not Slovakian!"

The Romanian officer stared at them helplessly, scratched his head, and beckoned them both to leave. The two of them were free to go. It was a happy ending! My grandpa made it home, and the story has become one of the success stories of the family. Especially because that very weekend, the Allies bombed the camp to the ground, so there would have been nowhere to return to anyway.

I'm sure that there are lots of war stories with the same message as ours. My grandfather took a risk and won. Of course, we don't have to go back in time as far as WWII to prove that we need to take some risks to gain success, develop further, or even just survive. The same applies to business life. It takes courage and fearlessness to be able to bluff in the business world, too. Think of a marketing or an acquisition meeting. I don't have to carry on explaining, do I?

> **Sometimes you need to attack, sometimes take defensive measures—but sometimes, bluffing is enough.**

2.15 GUEST STORY

From Belief to Proving:
the Beginning of the Road
Patrik Kovács
President
National Association of Young Entrepreneurs, Hungary and President of JEUNE – Young Entrepreneurs' Organization of the European Union

It's hard to beat a person who never gives up.—Babe Ruth

When I traveled to Mexico for the first time in my life, an experience made me understand more about the nature of success. It was a fantastic opportunity to be able to represent the European Union at the G20 Young Entrepreneurs Summit and make a million-dollar cooperation agreement of major economic and diplomatic importance with the Mexican Young Entrepreneurs Alliance; yet there was even more to why I felt so different when I arrived. I discovered something that gave me more strength to attain my goals.

The world's largest shrine of the Virgin of Guadalupe is situated in Mexico City. Pilgrims from all corners of the world come here to pay a visit once a year, eight million of them at the same time. It is deeply ingrained in the public psyche; only a few other things in the world have such an unquestionable degree of influence.

To be honest, the atmosphere blew me away too, and that's why I asked myself: what is the story of this place, how has it become so important? What is the force that has triggered so many people, persons who will spare no effort, to make a pilgrimage here?

The answer partially came from our local driver. This all began when in the sixteenth century, the Virgin Mary appeared to a young man, Juan Diego, at this place. Even though I misunderstood much of the driver's story in his broken English, it got me interested enough to actually read the whole story later on.

I suddenly realized that the "process" going with this old miracle has similarities with how a new enterprise starts off when a new initiative is picked up and how an organization starts operating in the world of economics.

I tried to imagine the path this young man might have taken, what difficulties he might have encountered, and I knew it was similar to what someone who wishes to build up a business enterprise goes through.

Really and truly, what's behind a start-up company or the National Alliance of Young Entrepreneurs is the same as what used to be behind this place: one or more people for whom something is true and important.

It makes no difference in this sense whether, back then, Juan wanted to prove to the world that something holy had happened to him or, today, the owner of a start-up company wishes to show that his idea will move the wheels of the world forward—or, as in my case, I wanted to establish a new economic union. Our goals are the same!

I imagined how the young man gave voice to what sort of miracle had happened to him and how important it was, wherever he went. I suppose people were suspicious and not everybody believed his story. Usually, few people believe in new ideas until it is proven to them that these are indeed valuable ideas, products, services, or perhaps a just cause. All beginnings are difficult, and the outcome depends on the perseverance, strength, and devotedness of the founders to show the world that what they believe in is indeed worth doing.

The skepticism of society can only be conquered if you prove your own strength to the world. The owner of a start-up company produces a prototype that the investor can physically handle, an organization begins to attain a critical mass, or, as in the story above, Juan starts to build a chapel with his own two hands. It doesn't matter as long as it's convincing!

This is one of the hardest tasks, and this is where most business ideas, start-ups, and projects fail: to prove ourselves without being able to rely on anyone, and to know throughout sleepless nights and long months or years that there are only two things to hang on to—ourselves and our objectives.

However, if we work with humility and endurance, our ideas will come to a turning point sooner or later, and as soon as we have enough evidence to present to the world, all of a sudden people will start believing in us and things will speed up.

When the first chapel was built at the place of the appearance in Mexico, when the prototype of a start-up was made, when the National Alliance of Young Entrepreneurs (FIVOSZ) in Hungary began to work together with an innumerable amount of youngsters and partners, people started to believe in what and who they had doubted beforehand. People who wanted to help started appearing and everything accelerated, becoming easier. It is a special feeling to experience and a privilege of a few.

This recognition has become embedded deep within me and has given me strength to stick by my beliefs. The road that leads to great things starts as a path, one that is long and rough, but behind every success there is a similar miracle.

At the place where once the Virgin Mary appeared, today a monumental complex stands, attracting millions of people. Similarities can be drawn here with how Bill Gates created Windows in a garage, for instance. A start-up project or enterprise can only be successful if the founders are devoted enough and are capable of persevering on the toughest part of the route: the beginning.

This part is full of challenges and uncertainty, yet "it's very hard to defeat the person who never gives up."

CHAPTER 3
Spring: From Concept to Reality

3.1   THE MESSAGE OF *THE POLAR EXPRESS*

When you change the thought, your reality must follow suit.
—Abraham Hicks

I love films. They are recreational and thought-provoking at the same time. Just as when I read a good book, I look out to find messages that are relevant to me, which I can utilize here and now. I was doing the same when I watched *The Polar Express*, directed by Robert Zemeckis. The protagonist is a cynical and somewhat nonbelieving ten-year-old who is not sure whether Santa Claus really exists; he believes that all the presents are placed underneath the Christmas tree by his parents. On the night of Christmas Eve, however, our hero is awakened by screeching and chugging sounds. Outside his house, in the middle of the night, in the snowy street, a huge steam locomotive pulls up. The conductor tells him that they've come to pick him up.

The boy rubs his eyes in disbelief; he thinks he is perhaps dreaming. After pondering for a moment, he boards the train. The steam engine slowly sets off, and a magical journey begins, one that changes his whole life and his way of thinking. The Polar Express, filled with other children in nighties and pajamas, is heading for the North Pole so that the children can meet Santa Claus and the elves. Of course, nothing goes that smoothly, for a little adventure and danger is necessary in every film, but collaboration eventually solves things.

Doubts, faith, seemingly unconquerable obstacles, inner tension, happiness, ups and downs—a great range of feelings is demonstrated in this film, and that's what makes this children's tale realistic. *The Polar Express* is like an enterprise. It is like launching a new project or strategy. You know what your goal is, but you have no idea what awaits you once you've boarded the train and it starts rolling on the track of implementation. It's natural to have some doubts, but you need to have faith and devotion, for there will be unforeseeable, unexpected obstacles along the way. You are not obligated to get on the train, just as it's not compulsory to stay at a company; but once you've boarded the company train, while you are on it, you take on the objectives of the firm. You have to be committed and able to deal with unexpected situations, as well as sometimes be in a race against time to achieve required results.

Running a company is like driving the Express. We are entrusted with taking it to the final destination. The conditions are given, but circumstances may change. A quantity of small and also important and complex tasks must be handled. You have to gain and keep the confidence of the owners. This is only possible, of course, if you carry through what you have taken on and meet your objectives, for which you need a suitable team. It is the manager's job to choose eligible employees, persons who can make the company operate even in difficult times, to sit beside him on the train.

A few months had passed since my appointment, and the end of the year was approaching. It had been a tradition for years to hold an end-of-year meeting for management, which included a short annual evaluation followed by a festive dinner. I was wondering whether this was necessary and, if so, what form it should take. We'd had several detailed discussions about our performance at our regular meetings during the year. We might be able to end the year—on our last working day—with something different. People would be concentrating more on the approaching festivities than wishing to analyze the boring data of the firm's annual results. I started thinking:

if we have this end-of-year meeting, what do we need to discuss? What is it that connects us as colleagues besides the results of the work we share?

I talked to several of my colleagues about this, and I got a variety of opinions. I don't know to this day when the idea actually sprang to mind, but it was *The Polar Express* that triggered it. I decided to go ahead with the meeting but to make it rather unconventional. We wouldn't talk about the tasks ahead in the conventional way but with the aid of creative works, ones analyzed from the point of view of the manager that could provide useful experiences regarding people's work. It could be a film or part of a novel, and something that reminds us of the festivities too.

Just like the young boy who boards the Polar Express, managers face new challenges and new tasks at the beginning of any new year. Delivering my message in such an uncommon way, using elements connected to the festivities, helped embed these things in my colleagues' minds much more deeply. Here is what I had to say: "Our enterprise is an express train—it is not compulsory that someone boards it and stays on it, but it is worth doing so. Whoever shares a ride with us should be a worthy member of the team. He or she should fight for the team's mutual success and appreciate the achieved results."

We were preparing for important changes. These projects were going to be of major significance in the following years. Not many people knew about these plans at the firm because some of the details had not been clarified. The end-of-year meeting was the best opportunity to invite all employees onto this journey into the future, aboard the express train of the company. I prepared a short introduction, highlighting the new opportunities and summarizing tasks, omitting all unnecessary figures, and using lots of pictures instead.

I told my colleagues, "I'm inviting everyone on an unusual journey now, a few days before Christmas," as the noisy Polar Express train from the film appeared on the screen. "Get on board!" I shouted, along with the conductor. "Our adventure is about to begin! Let's look around to see what doors might be opening up for us and what experiences we might gain in the years to come." My colleagues took on board what I was saying and "got on the train"—and company fluctuations in the managerial and expert positions were practically nonexistent in the following year.

Upon waking up the next morning, the little boy seriously doubts whether he has really been a part of this big adventure and has almost started to think that it was only a dream—until he finds the train ticket in his pocket. We often react the same way. We will always have new objectives that sometimes bring about great changes. We set out and reach a particular station on our train. Our journey is sometimes paved with success and sometimes with failure, yet if we like the team we are part of and the firm we are working for, we will have no doubts about whether the ticket for the Polar Express is in our pocket or not.

We should carry through what we embark upon and shouldn't get off when we are only halfway there.

3.2 WHAT IS IMPORTANT AND BENEFICIAL

Failure is simply the opportunity to begin again,
this time more intelligently.
—Henry Ford

Julien Mantle is a high-flying lawyer who owns an island, an airplane, and a Ferrari. He burns the candle at both ends, and at the age of fifty-three, he looks like a seventy-year-old. His distressed and troubled lifestyle almost leads to a fatal heart attack. Mantle is given another chance at life, which he intends to use wisely. He sells all his possessions, quits his profitable job at the law firm, and sets off for India to find the meaning of life. Three years later, when he returns home, his friend John is surprised to see Julien's transformation: he looks like a man in his thirties.

During his spiritual journey in the Far East, Mantle learns from the wise and practical advice of the monks to effectively free his mental, physical, and spiritual abilities. Combining the way of thinking of the West and the philosophy of the East, Robin Sharma, the author of *The Monk Who Sold His Ferrari: A Fable About Fulfilling Your Dreams and Reaching Your Destiny*, shows readers how to live a more courageous, more balanced, and more content life.

Managing one's time is a hard business. We take on each task enthusiastically and full of energy after obtaining our university degree. Then we realize, all of a sudden, that we are getting home late from work on a regular basis, and we don't have time to spare for our families, sports activities, or relaxation. If there is an employee evaluation and we talk about our problems, the person responsible for human resources will be eager to take notes—and will then come up with the following: "We need to organize a time-management training." We have, of course, also thought about this.

The first book I read on the topic was *The Ten Natural Laws of Successful Time and Life Management* by Hyrum Smith. This book has helped me a great deal, and I often page through it even today. Hyrum Smith first talks about life ambitions in his book; they need to be intelligent. When we have set these, the next step is to take a regular fifteen-minute break every day to organize our schedule. We need to prioritize tasks according to their importance while always keeping our long-term objectives in mind. However, this is more than a simple time-management reference book—it helps us take control of our lives.

Stephen R. Covey also deals with time management in his book *The Seven Habits of Highly Effective People*, which has sold more than 20 million copies. The author differentiates between four types of time-management strategies: the first one is based on checklists; the second is use of a daily planner, such as a Day-Timer or Filofax; the third is supplementing the previous two with priorities; and the fourth introduces the matrix of importance and urgency. With this, we'll be able to decide in what time frame we would like to carry out tasks according to possibilities of attaining results and not only according to ranking. Tasks are classified in the four quarters of the matrix as follows: important/urgent, important/not urgent, not important/urgent, and not important/not urgent. Productive people keep away from the third and fourth quarters. We need to be able to say no so that we can do this. One can also find clever solutions for this in the book.

I came across another interesting book on the topic recently: *Bear Strategy: Power through Calmness* by Lothar Seiwert. According to the bear strategy, every day is a happy day, and tranquility is power itself—the symbol of which is the bear. We can learn a few "bear virtues" from Seiwert, such as how to find our goal in life or the principle of doing what we feel like most, and doing those things for which we have the best abilities.

Heaps of good advice, but at the end of the day all of these books warn us about the basics: we need to find the purpose of our lives and live in a balanced way. For some of us, this means eight hours of work, eight hours rest, and eight hours of recreation; for others, leading a balanced life may have different proportions. We should be aware of this, for our time is limited.

> **The order of your tasks should be decided upon by their importance or urgency, but you should never lose sight of how significant they are in achieving your life's goal.**

3.3 BELIEVE IN YOUR DREAMS!

All our dreams can come true,
if we have the courage to pursue them.
—*Walt Disney*

In my opinion, the fairly typically American quote from Walt Disney above has a serious meaning, one that I have experienced more than once. If we believe in our dreams, they will come true. We have to take action, of course, and should never give up. Our dreams are our goals, which will never be attained unless we do something in order to achieve them. You need perseverance and will to make your dreams come true. A Taoist poem comes to mind: "Don't rush and don't hasten—everything in its own time."

It's been almost twenty years since I became acquainted with a unique entrepreneur. He was past his prime by then. He proudly showed me the products of his company at this first meeting. Product samples, award certificates, acknowledgments—the foyer of his office was a little museum. Still under the spell of my university years, I could only see the future in terms of computers. Yet he was talking to me about something completely different: hip-replacement prosthetics. "This is incomparable in Hungary," he said, "and a local development." Later, he asked, "A daring undertaking, isn't it?"

He took me on a tour of the factory—there were about fifty people working there at the time—and he told me his story. He had started fifteen years earlier as a car mechanic but had always dreamed about making implants. He read about them, tried things out, looked for connections, and after some years of hard work, his first products were born. These were followed by new ways of doing things. Products became product families, several being patented, and there were life-improving advancements. Phenomenal results were achieved that might have seemed unattainable at the beginning. His dream came true because it was paired with a strong will, faith, perseverance, and a professional humility. All of these helped him overcome the obstacles.

When a hip joint becomes unhealthy, it causes great pain and restricted movement. The cure lies in an operation: doctors replace the damaged joint with a prosthesis. My acquaintance learned everything possible about this malady, analyzed all firms producing hip-replacement prostheses, and also studied related solutions and production technologies. He threw himself into making his dream come true. It was a complete change of career path, and with no ordinary challenge! He began his own development, and success was soon to follow as mass production began.

By the time we'd walked through the factory, I was completely captivated by his enthusiasm as he talked about the products and new developments. The production technology was based on the most modern computer-operated machinery. I saw at least as many new products as the number of new ideas and new directions he told me of. I felt as if I was in a research laboratory. I was looking for a job at the time, but we had merely met on the off chance. Of course, we also referred to this during our conversation.

"Would you like to work for me?" he asked. "For we are preparing a computer-aided design system at the moment." I didn't hesitate for long. I was interested in what I saw, and above all, I would be overseeing the information-technology developments.

As luck would have it, I only worked at the firm for a year, yet I came to learn during this time that he was an outstanding person and a great expert in his field. Our working relationship didn't last long, though our friendship did, and I was always happy to meet up and have a chat. He is no longer among us, but the example he set and the work he has done still inspires respect in people today.

> **You won't necessarily become successful having faith and persistence, but without them, you will certainly fail.**

3.4 THE GOOD AND THE BAD

> Do *what you believe in and believe in what you do.*
> *Everything else is only a waste of energy and time.*
> —*Nisargadatta Maharaj*

Is it usually easy to decide who is good and who is bad when you read a tale? When you watch the unforgettable *Peter Pan* cartoon, you instantly know that the pirate captain is the evil one. Watching *Snow White and the Huntsman* (based on the fairy tale "Snow White"), however, we wonder whether the queen represents evil or whether she is a victim.

With economic enterprises, one does not need to differentiate between good and bad, yet it is important to know what your responsibilities and your tasks are. Smaller economic enterprises don't often have to face this issue, as it is the managing director who decides on the structure of the organization, and he probably knows everyone. Whatever such a small enterprise is like, owing to its size everyone knows very well what the tasks and responsibilities are; this is all transparent. As a result, if things are not working out in a given field, the problem can be identified practically straight away, and the person responsible can be found.

In a global environment, and in the case of firms operating as holdings, because of differences in the interests of local, regional, and global functional fields, there will be many little confrontations. It is almost impossible to find the point of origin of a wrong decision and why it became such in practice. This would be one of the smaller problems. The issue is not that it occurs, it is whether an organization can draw conclusions from this, can make amendments, and can take action so that it won't happen again. As one of Toyota's basic company-managing perspectives puts it: "One should bring about a continuous process flow that brings problems to the surface."

Toyota's objective is fewer working hours, smaller stock, and the best quality cars on the market. In order to achieve this, the company is constantly raising standards regarding production, product development, and the quality of procedures. The outcome has been an overwhelming business success, with increasing market share, a growing profit, and globally acknowledged results among business managers. Meanwhile, their competitors seek to compete by lowering their prices.

The Toyota Lean system has triggered a revolution in both industrial and service companies. With this, a new era—beyond the era of mass production—has begun. The Toyota production system is a type of management philosophy that, relying on continual development and learning as well as building a culture by which one makes quality goods, aims at avoiding loss by fully satisfying customer expectations. Bosses are trained within the company, they help their employees improve, and they teach them problem-solving. Believing in the principle of mutual advantage, employees here grow and develop along with their suppliers and partners. The method has been taken on and applied by lots of other companies. The question is: what must one pay attention to so that the technique could be instrumental in a company culture that differs from Japan's?

Having gained several years' experience, Thomas was appointed manager of production and product development in the Serbian subsidiary, his firm's flagship production base in Eastern Europe. Thomas was overwhelmed by such an opportunity. He had worked in several different positions within the company group but had never had both production and product development under his wing. The Serbian factory, because of its geographical location, held a strategically important position. There were plans to create a base there for Eastern European expansion, in which Thomas would have an important role.

Thomas's tasks included preparing the local team for new projects and for the major increases in workload that would come. John, who came to work for the company HQ almost at the same time as Thomas as a company group "outsider," was assigned the responsible position of managing the company's foreign affiliates. After his appointment, he visited the European manufacturers. During these visits, they updated their business plans. When John met Thomas, he reported the following: "The present production system of the group is not competitive enough—the future is the Lean way. The subsidiary that acts first will gain a competitive advantage against others."

Thomas had been toying with introducing the Lean pilot system idea for a long time, yet the previous management hadn't supported him. *Superb*, he thought. *It's great that John has come to work for the company group from the outside, otherwise changes wouldn't take place so quickly.* "I'm really grateful for this opportunity. I have already been thinking about it," he said to John, who suggested that Thomas visit England, where he could gain some experience from their latest acquisition, a company operating on the basis of Lean principles.

Thomas was in a difficult position, though, for a mere half a year earlier the head office had set different priorities. It seemed as if they had spent lots of money on expensive training for one part of the team, but in vain. He wondered if people would understand what this complete turnaround was about. Yet he was driven by his curiosity. He had read a great deal about Lean methods, and he believed that this was the future.

He returned from the English subsidiary with mixed feelings. He saw a company much smaller than the one in Serbia, with a narrower product portfolio. The methods they had introduced seemed to be effective, and their theoretical approach and points of view concerning processes matched those he had already experienced. Both the management and employees got involved in procedures and moved in the direction of increasing efficiency. It was in their mutual interest to improve competitiveness. Supplying customer needs and the elimination of losses were the two main objectives. At the same time, Thomas felt that the English subsidiary, in spite of having had several years of experience, didn't always choose the most suitable solutions to problems. This was only intuition, though.

Upon returning home, Thomas studied the available reference material introducing Lean management and the Kaizen method. The basic principle is that the company with all its employees, from manager to labor, "has to concentrate on value-generating processes." All processes that do not represent value to the customer or that cannot be converted into value are superfluous—that is, they create loss. Such processes may arise anywhere, and it is the responsibility of all employees to eliminate them. This often means reevaluating and reorganizing processes, and this can only be implemented by involving each and every employee, as only those persons who carry out specific work processes will know their minute details.

This method has been developed by combining American and Japanese work-organization methods. There is a vital issue here that many overlook: as a result of increased efficiency owing to reorganization, there will be some excess capacity, which can lead to an excess of production, so the production cost per unit will show a reduction. If savings means job cuts, this will be the death of the process. We will lose the most valuable resource, the innovation-motivated employee, for nobody wants to put a noose around his or her own neck.

Thomas had hardly returned from the English subsidiary when a new project was launched. Subsidiaries had to try to save on costs in line with the "produce or outsource" principle. His immediate superior was supportive of the Lean project that Thomas was thinking about; he even wanted to—based on the success story of the English subsidiary—introduce it into other subsidiaries. This would have been an enormous success story for Thomas and his team if, in parallel with this, central project-encouraging outsourcing hadn't begun, which would probably lead to job cuts. Lean produces an increased capacity that generates a rising number of jobs, and then specific expenses can be reduced. To make things even more complicated for Thomas, and the challenge even greater, a decision was made about a transfer project at a group level, which the Serbian subsidiary won. This meant a significant amount of investment and increased capacity.

Thomas mulled over the issue for a while. He had to find the right response to this dilemma. Finally, he came up with one. He suggested introducing the Lean pilot project as a priority. He figured out the workload with reference to the increased internal capacity and the new project. The outsourcing proposal was based on these factors. Thus, it was not only owing to the Lean project that a specific capacity increase was able to occur; the new project was also able to be relocated to Serbia in a cost-effective way via reorganizing the increased capacity and the amount of external/internal workload. By scheduling the introduction of projects for different times, the Lean project also led to increased efficiency, while savings were noticeable in connection with the outsourcing project. All of this happened without the need to change the number of technical staff members.

To Thomas's point of view, this was a win-win situation. Because of declining operational expenses, the company group's products were becoming more competitive. Employees remained motivated, and there were no job cuts. Outsourcing production had lowered the demand for investment. The sacrifices made and the time invested in finding the optimum solution had paid off. As Bruce Pandolfini writes in his book *Every Move Must Have a Purpose: Strategies from*

Chess for Business and Life, "We should only make sacrifices if we can certainly gain an advantage this way."

The following year, Thomas was facing new challenges. His boss set him a new task: given the successes so far, he had to find new subcontractors for use with the introduction of a new product family. The new task was manifold. The group had already found a new cooperating partner in Slovenia and had come to a decision. Thomas made several attempts to object at various meetings, bringing forth several rational reasons for these as, utilizing the overheads and risk principles, it would have been much more beneficial to implement the project with the already-existing Serbian subcontractor. His suggestion was rejected; people decided they wanted this new cooperating partner and withdrew the assignment from Thomas. They entrusted the management of the project, nicknamed Salsa, to a manager from the head office.

Thomas overheard at times that things weren't going too well, but he didn't care much anymore. The Serbian subsidiary produced great results. They had a well-organized, motivated team, and to work together with such people was a real joy. At the following year's budget presentation, Thomas was informed that, even though the Salsa project did have its minor defects, the project phase had ended and the Serbian-affiliated enterprise was going to be a part of his portfolio. He realized when he took things over that the Salsa project's drawbacks were not small but serious. The Slovenian supplier had miscalculated its expenses, so it was working for a much higher price than had originally been quoted. This resulted in significantly higher costs, yet the contracts didn't allow for this problem to be solved—otherwise, they would've had to make an outlay of a more notable sum of money.

At the following meeting, Thomas brought the subject up with his boss, but he wasn't particularly successful. By assigning this activity to him, his boss had ruined the performance of the Serbian subsidiary. Thomas asked him to make an evaluation of the two different areas of activity separately. The suggestion was finally accepted, although the boss wasn't overly impressed when Thomas called it a lose-lose situation.

Everyone is responsible for implementing a solution that is of value to the client, but if there is no one to blame for delays in the process, it's time to get your own house in order.

3.5 MANAGERS AND OBJECTIVES

Try not to become a man of success,
but rather try to become a man of value.
—*Albert Einstein*

In 1975, Margaret Thatcher became the first female head of the British Conservative Party. In her speech at the party conference after her election, she explained the new policy of the Tories. The speech had been difficult to formulate. Sir Ronald Millar, Thatcher's primary speech writer, only finished writing the speech at five in the morning, because she had kept suggesting alterations.

"Oh, no, this is not correct at all!" she'd say.

"What's the matter with it?" asked Millar.

"This is not me, my dear," she replied.

In her speech, she put into words her vision of the country built on British traditions: "Let me give you my vision. A man's right to work as he will, to spend what he earns, to own property, to have the State as servant and not as master: these are the British inheritance." The speech was interrupted several times with ovations and cheering. Be it a country or a company, the vision and the mission sets the direction and lays out the long-term objectives—like a lighthouse that signals to ships moving across the ocean, "This way, the harbor is here!" Just like a ship on the ocean, a business also encounters plenty of unexpected situations. In foggy and stormy conditions, the role of the lighthouse becomes even more important.

Our vision helps us stay on the right path. It gives a decision-making scope both to managers and employees. Nevertheless, we make our decisions based on guiding values formed within us. Values like integrity, affection, and honesty are determining elements of our personality. There are personal goals that we set for ourselves in order to have self-fulfillment. These guiding principles determine who we are. Our values might change during the course of our lives, depending on influences. Even though our guiding principles are also our most important priorities when we make any decision, there may be a big difference between reality and our ideals.

We need to clarify what goals and values are driving us if we want to improve the quality of our lives. Abraham Maslow called the correspondence between our values and our everyday activities "self-fulfillment." According to Hyrum Smyth, the greater the correspondence between our decisions and values, the better our performance and inner sense of fulfillment, our "inner peace."

Credibility is perhaps the most important, fundamental value for a manager. I say what I do, and I do as I say. This forms part of the basic values of many companies—except that the task of the manager appointed by the owner is to ensure that the owner's interests and annual objectives are looked after. Giving the owner value is an interesting issue, since it may clash with the values held by the actual manager. Anything can be taken on, yet the question is whether it is worth sacrificing our inner peace and credibility. It's a difficult decision to make, but sometimes senior managers don't give in; they would rather resign than give up values and objectives that they believe in.

Such an event occurred when on the last day of March 2011, the managing director of Acer, Gianfranco Lanci, who had been managing the firm since 2005, unexpectedly quit. This professional explained his resignation by saying that he didn't agree with the course of action the management wished to pursue in the coming years. Similarly, when Péter Felcsuti, the managing director of Raiffeisen Bank, resigned from his post as chairman of the Hungarian Banking Association in the middle of September 2009, the reason given was that he didn't agree with the opinion of a few dominant members of the association in relation to the banking code of conduct.

Many differences of opinion may occur between the objectives and values of senior managers and the proprietor; perhaps most of them never come to light, either, though one particular assessment is revealing. Researchers from Canada's Laval University had been investigating for years what serves to motivate a senior manager's transition from one job to another. Research results showed that one third of senior managers change jobs because they have a misunderstanding with either the owners or a new, most of the time nonprofessional, investor.

Conflict between the fulfilling of proprietary values and the personal values of the manager is, fortunately, not an everyday issue. The accomplishment of annual objectives is very much an everyday task of the manager, though, and these are usually the measures and annual objectives for sales turnover, expenses, investment, and profit. Objectives like these are never easy to achieve, but it is even more difficult to face up to our fears in tougher economic circumstances.

The story of Gita Mehta's book *Raj* takes place in India, far away from Europe. In the point of view of certain critics, there hasn't since *Gone With the Wind* been another novel in which imagination and history intertwine in such a fascinating way. Jaya Singh, born as a princess into the traditional household of the royal family of Balmer, has to fight history if she wants to fulfill her task of protecting her people. Jaya, battling between the conceptions of tradition and those of Mahatma Gandhi, becomes an alert politician who leads her kingdom to victory in an insidiously changing world. I have chosen to quote the following—exceptional—part of Chapter 1:

> On a cold, January morning the five-year-old Jaya was taken to the jungle by her father ... The dew of the night hadn't yet evaporated. The sunshine made its way through the cobwebs covering the prickly bushes, which antelopes were nibbling on. Jaya shouted out in trepidation. She saw through the undergrowth that her father and his men had come face to face with a black panther, chained to a shala tree. The animal pulled on the steel links of the chain, blood started running down his neck, his furious roar filled the

jungle. Jaya held on to the shikari and kept her eyes closed, even when somebody lifted her up and took her closer to the sound. When she finally gained enough courage to open her eyes, she was only standing about thirty centimetres away from the roaring animal. She wanted to hide behind her father's legs but Jai Singh peeled her fingers off and turned her towards the panther ... Monarchs are also people, and people are always afraid, but only those who face their fears will be able to rule.

I still believe this thought to be true: managers have to be able to face their fears and doubts calmly, otherwise they will never become good leaders.

According to American civil-rights leader Benjamin Elijah Mays, "The tragedy of life doesn't lie in not reaching your goal. The tragedy lies in having no goal to reach." I share this view. We are allowed to have doubts and fears to achieve our goals, but we do have to look them in the eye and concentrate on solving the tasks that can aid our achievement. At the same time, we should insist on our guiding values because, even though it's difficult, for our credibility it is at times worth saying no to shareholders.

Only take on what you yourself value, and if necessary, face your fears.

3.6 IF IT DOESN'T WORK, THINK OF SOMETHING DIFFERENT

The heart has its reasons, which reason does not know.
—Pascal

When we set ourselves some objectives or need to meet some at work, we typically believe that we will be able to fulfill them. We do everything in order to do so. Yet there often comes a time when we begin to suspect we may fail. These are difficult situations. We become discouraged, although it seems we have still done everything possible to attain our goal. The question is, how long can we keep on going? When will we start slowing down? When do we reach the point when the lessons or musings within us, along with our despondency, make us give up?

In project management they call this phase, the one that we normally reach at the beginning of the last third on the time scale of project implementation, the phase of uncertainties. That's when the project manager and his or her team begin to think that they might not be able to finish on time what they have taken on. This is the time when we mustn't give up, though. We have to face the panther! We have to face our fears and handle them, but we must also keep our eyes on the objective.

Managing our uncertainties means managing our heart's debates. We have to find something else that will inspire and motivate us— something that will provide some compensation and charge us up for the delayed sense of achieving success. You have to be like a hybrid vehicle that uses two power sources to move, one of them usually being a diesel engine and the other an electric motor. It is the car's electronics system that decides which one is more economical to use at any given time.

You also need to find a solution through which you can gain some sense of achievement, which is necessary to keep up your inner motivation, from two or more different resources. If one of the resources essential for reaching your heightened goal starts running low, you can charge yourself up from the other one. You will gather strength from the success of another project, a friendly chat, or some recreational activity done. Of course, your family can also be an incredibly beneficial resource.

Péter Rajna, a neurologist and psychiatrist, elaborates in his book *Black Sheep and White Ravens* on how our interests change throughout our lifetime. In parallel with the activity of earning a living, other preoccupations become strengthened. These will often be recreational activities or hobbies that you have done before. Rajna describes this as being partly due to increased recreational time and partly because, as we gain more experience at work, we feel less of a challenge. On the basis of these factors, we could say that this happens more frequently at certain times in our career.

At the end of the day, it makes no difference whether we deliberately try to find an alternative resource to keep our motivation at its peak or it just happens because of changing circumstances in our way of life. The point is to find challenges and objectives from which we can get enough positive energy to charge up our inner battery. Switching off temporarily from our everyday routine and distractions can often help us realize what is stopping us from reaching our goals in the context of an important project. If we try to solve our problems less doggedly and look at them from different angles—perhaps even as an outsider—we will instantly realize the right next step to take that will deliver success.

If you get stuck, step outside for a moment and then start over again—but don't give up.

3.7   FACTS AND LESSONS TO BE LEARNED FROM THE ANIMAL WORLD

By loving and understanding animals, perhaps we humans shall come to understand each other.
—Dr. Louis J. Camuti

Sometimes it is worth observing animals. Many a technical innovation has come into being based on ideas brought forth from the world of animals. Can their behavior and cognitive abilities also possibly provide useful ideas?

The article "Myths and Reality Concerning the Intelligence of Dolphins" by Csaba Molnár looks at, among other things, the communication of these aquatic mammals. The whistling and chirping of dolphins serves to help their orientation; as with bats, it serves as an ultrasound locator. The whistling sounds also serve as a form of communication:

> These whistling sounds are short—lasting only one second; they are high-pitched sounds, which are unique to each dolphin. To examine the information encoded in such whistles, Laela Sayigh, researcher of the University of North Carolina, recorded some identifying whistles. Based

on these, and with the aid of a computer, she managed to recreate a synthetic whistling. Their melody was the same as the real ones', though they didn't contain naturally generated elements coming via the body characteristics of each dolphin, whence differences arise between them. They then played these synthetic noises to fourteen dolphins to find out if the dolphins listened to the whistles recreated using the original sounds made by their close relatives— and they turned toward the loudspeaker more often in this case than if they were hearing the synthesized whistles of unknown dolphins. This could only have been possible if they recognized the sounds made by their relatives.

It is likely then (researchers assume) that dolphins consciously identify themselves with their group mates.

Perhaps this article about dolphins doesn't surprise us, but what's the situation with wild geese? Do they have cognitive abilities as well? Let's have a look:

- *Fact:* Canada geese fly in a V-shaped formation. As they move their wings up and down, they reduce wind resistance and trail air turbulence, so that it becomes easier for the geese following them to hold themselves up in the air. This is how they can cover a 71 percent longer distance than if only one pair was flying.
- *Lesson to be learned:* If we help each other at work, we will be more effective and will achieve our objectives more rapidly.
- *Fact:* If a goose gets out of line and tries to reach his destination alone, he will slow down immediately because the lifting effect of the air generated by the movement of his companions' wings ceases to exist. He quickly returns to his place in line so that he can fly more easily again, with the aid of the others.
- *Lesson to be learned:* If we have as much sense as a Canada goose, we will work together with our community for mutual success.

- *Fact:* When the leading goose gets tired, another one takes its place.
- *Lesson to be learned:* We have to accept that we depend on each other when in a community, and at a crucial moment we may have to take on or hand over a task—even, from time to time, the leading role.
- *Fact:* While flying, geese at the back try to encourage those in the front in their efforts with a loud honking.
- *Lesson to be learned:* A community cannot exist without supporters, and it's important for any honking to be an encouraging thing.
- *Fact:* When a goose becomes ill, two of his partners land with him, and they will remain together either until he gets better or until he dies. The geese, either only two of them or all three, then return to their own community. They may fly with another group of geese until they reach their own group.
- *Lesson to be learned:* If we were as empathetic as wild geese, we would help each other in hard times as they do.

In my opinion, based on the above, if a team were to "take off" like the Canada geese, it would be a phenomenal performance.

3.8   COMMUNICATIONAL BLACK HOLES

When I am getting ready to reason with a man, I spend one-third of my time thinking about myself and what I am going to say and two-thirds about him and what he is going to say.
—Abraham Lincoln

There are many different factors that can determine how efficiently a company's communication system operates. These include:

- company cultures
- through which channel internal and external information reaches employees and how detailed it is

- what the company's hierarchy is like
- how open and honest communication is
- the boss-employee relationship
- the size of the firm
- what type of activity the firm is involved in
- how much information the management wants to share with employees

The question is whether it is worth spending time on these things. Will it help a company along if we get to know it more accurately? If we start with the assumption that precise communication of our decisions is required for appropriate implementation and that the perception of decisions affects people's attitudes and therefore performance, then the answer can only be yes. It is important for a company to know and utilize its instruments of communication. And if we take into account the fact that a company and circumstances are constantly changing, it is worth reconsidering external and internal communicational strategies from time to time.

Most of the black holes in any information flow are formed when a certain decision made by senior management has to be communicated; the language and measures used in describing company strategy objectives can be hard to comprehend, and it's also difficult to see what performance expectations related to some given field will be. It has to be clear to all employees where the company is heading and what each employee's—and also the team's—role will be in the implementing of objectives. Unfortunately, employees often only receive partial information concerning a decision or are allowed to see not entirely suitable or accurate cause-effect relationships. I have experienced this myself. It happened barely a year ago.

We regularly renegotiate our contracts with different service providers. After our last tendering, we managed to agree on a more favorable tariff package with our mobile service provider. We transferred the cheaper tariff into our system and were able to reduce the (separate) budget for making phone calls. It wasn't our intention to reduce the talking time available; the limit values only changed as much as the new, more favorable per-minute prices justified. As a direct result, work colleagues were able to talk for an equal amount of time when making calls of the same composition even though their monthly limit had been reduced.

We did inform our colleagues of this, but only the "bad news" registered—that their monthly limit had been cut. Everyone was complaining and moaning, and they gossiped in the corridors about why their limits had been changed. The demotivation factor, a result of the communicational black hole that had actually swallowed the point it was making, caused a loss of work hours and perhaps even some loss of sales turnover. We had to release some additional information so things would calm down. Instead of putting an emphasis on the result, we should have highlighted the fact that the time limit hadn't changed, it was just that we'd negotiated a more favorable tariff.

The lesson to be learned from this story is that all messages to be conveyed have to be planned, regardless of the reason for the communication. One needs to know exactly what one wants to say, and how. In certain cases, it is productive to draw up an action plan in which you list your tasks, the time frame required to implement them, the target audience, deadlines, and other available details. After the communication, be it an oral or a written message, we should try to evaluate its impact. This is an important step, because formal and informal internal communications exist side by side. Informal communication might indeed suppress formal communication if the latter channel is not so efficient.

Vocal colleagues whose opinion should be listened to by persons dealing with internal communication exist everywhere, and they can significantly strengthen or weaken official, formal communications. This can either increase or decrease the commitment of employees, which may indirectly affect performance. Existing business objectives might be hung up on the wall in vain, as employees see corridor gossip as being a more reliable source of information than documents signed by the managing director.

A communicational black hole is not only a result of faulty communication; unobserved informal channels might also be causing it as the two can directly affect each other. Studies by three American researchers—Rob Cross, Nitin Nohria, and Andrew Parker—reveal that the current organizational culture, which has become more open in the last few decades, has helped to strengthen the influencing effects of informal communicational channels. This is exactly what the new field of organizational network analysis studies, using knowledge from psychology, sociology, mathematics, anthropology, and business research. According to network-research reference literature, there are informational centers in every organization, so-called *coordinators*, who connect colleagues within the context of the internal workings of a given community; there are also *gatekeepers* who informally connect the organization to the outside world. Gatekeepers bring the information in from the outside.

In my view (and without underestimating the importance of the persons mentioned above), opinion leaders who can have a great deal of influence on the internal affairs of a company because of their connections are essential. To my mind, getting to know the opinion leaders is a vital aspect of internal-communication tactics. It might be beneficial to have experts draw up a map portraying information flow. The result here will be a map of the business network, showing who is at the center of the flow.

Even though we shouldn't, we are likely to underestimate the importance of communication. Apart from giving attention to the flow of information, we also have to observe *how* we communicate. Guy Kawasaki, in his book *Enchantment: The Art of Changing Hearts, Minds, and Actions*, uses convincing stories to prove that it is not enough to just possess a good idea in order to have success; we also need expertise or investor confidence. We need effective communication to achieve success—as Kawasaki calls it, "the art of enchantment"—by which we will be able to influence "hearts and minds."

To be able to have the desired effect, you need to know who your message will be for, and how to deliver it.

3.9 IF COOLING WATER BOILS ...

How do you know if something is good or bad, if something is
right or wrong? Only by making a decision. Decisions always
mean that the coin may fall on either side; and one can never be
100 percent sure that what you decide will be right. Sometimes
a wrong decision could be a helpful lesson, as you will then
value the good times and your right decisions much more.
—Sebastian Vettel

Most of us nowadays have a driver's license; there is no need to become a Formula 1 driver for this. Let's set off in the chaotic morning rush hour of a big city. Suppose we leave Cypress Hills in Brooklyn at seven fifteen in the morning and we are rushing toward to the Carnegie Hill neighborhood in Manhattan. We will drive in a different manner if we need to be there at nine compared to if we have to get there an hour earlier. And if we have to arrive by half past seven? Perhaps we won't even set out—we will first think things through, and then decide.

We are always being forced to make decisions that can determine the course of our lives, so it's important how we make them. We can either make good or bad ones; the latter can at times be corrected, yet we have to try to deliberately keep down the number of wrong decisions made. We will be able to reduce the proportion of bad decisions if we consider things beforehand. A smart decision means that we comprehensibly evaluate the information coming from our environment, without extreme emotion, from the point of view of reaching our goals.

A bad decision can often be traced back to one of three things:

1. We didn't deliberate.
2. The information available was not appropriate.
3. We didn't have a sufficient amount of information available on the given subject.

I believe we even deliberate when we are not aware of it. A good example of this is when, in a circle of friends, as a result of peer pressure, one of them does something without thinking things through, which he or she probably wouldn't have done under different circumstances, with time for consideration. We almost always realize later on that we have made a bad, overly hasty decision.

The second situation is one arising from a basis of incorrect data—for example, when the indicators on the dashboard of a car are faulty and are giving an erroneous message. You may then get a nasty surprise! The cooling water might boil over, for example, leading to a burnt-out engine, for you only realize what's going on when the car has already started belching smoke.

The third scenario is when, to carry on using the example of a car, there is no indicator on the dashboard at all that could warn us about the temperature of the water cooler.

The most frequent activity of a manager is, perhaps, decision-making. I have participated in company trainings often over the last twenty years, both at home and abroad. When manager traits were mentioned and we had to prioritize them, decision-making was always among the most important factors, often at the top of the list. However professional you are in this respect, it may occur that if the data available to you is incomplete or incorrect and you are pressed for time and so forced to take a hasty step, a bad decision will be made (with all its detrimental consequences).

Companies usually aim to be profitable. To simplify, if at the end of the year I deduct my expenses from turnover, I need to be left with a little profit. It will be very bad, though, if I only find out at the end of the year that there is nothing left. Larger companies that operate several different divisions will have separate objectives in every field. They measure the performance of a given field based on these factors. This way, they can define how efficiently each division is contributing to generating profit for the company overall.

Model Ltd. made lamps and kitchen equipment and had a fairly steady market share. Last year, however, imports from the Far East became ever more pronounced. Because of the stiffer price competition, lowering production costs became a priority. The production manager—let's call him Ottó—indicated at a meeting where the most important annual tasks were discussed that he had several ideas that might help to reduce costs a lot. He got the go-ahead and implemented several small changes in the factory, and also modified the production process. Changes in the shift system were also implemented by eliminating the third shift and moving its load to the first and second shifts.

In the monthly evaluation analyses of costs, by comparing the forecasted figures with actual ones, it was acknowledged that results were satisfactory, so making the changes was paying off. The figures showed that they had managed to achieve a 5 percent saving in overhead expenses. After the summer holidays, the August closing data was available too, and this took Ottó by surprise. Production's overhead expenses, instead of decreasing—as based on the aggregated data of the first eight months—had *increased* by two percent.

This is impossible, thought Ottó. *Our expenses have been under control up till now. We couldn't have become so counterproductive that we'd be using up months of savings.* After a lengthy investigation, it was discovered that a function in the software had been referring to an erroneous cell. Some expenses had been missing from the analysis from the beginning of the year owing to human error in end-of-year database maintenance. As an outcome, the "cooling water had come to the boil" undetected, and the machine was almost "emitting smoke" by the time the problem was revealed. Even though Ottó's team had seemingly made the right decision, they had been looking at factors on the basis of erroneous data.

Experience proves that from time to time, it is worth examining your data-collecting and -processing systems so that you don't make the same mistakes. You mustn't implicitly believe what the data shows, for that cooling water might just be coming to the boil.

The founder of judo, Kanō Jigorō, worked out the following five fundamental principles of the sport, which are cited in the book *Budo Secrets* by John Stevens:

1. Carefully observe oneself and one's situation, carefully observe others, and carefully observe one's environment.

2. Seize the initiative in whatever you undertake.
3. Consider fully, act decisively.
4. Know when to stop.
5. Keep to the middle.

Aren't these pieces of advice worth utilizing when one is making a decision?

Decide wisely!

3.10 THE MIGRATION OF VALUES

The only profit center is a customer whose check hasn't bounced.
—*Peter Drucker*

The Last Samurai is a film worth watching. The film's director, Edward Zwick, based his story on the 1876–77 Samurai rebellion. It is a watchable historical film that takes us into a world we Europeans are unaccustomed to. Japan entered mainstream history during the Meiji Restoration. After several decades of isolation, it was forced into a form of semicolonial dependency by foreign powers. After this isolation and a bloody change of regime, Japan rapidly caught up with developed Western technology. This critical period of time, from the point of view of the Samurai, is what the film depicts. One can see the clash of values on the screen, of the Samurai's conceptions and the new order now fighting a bloody battle with each other.

The means of operating that the opposing sides utilize are completely different, not only from the point of view of tactical weapons but economics and business as well. Economically, market opportunities for Samurai sword-makers were significantly reduced with the appearance and spread of new types of military equipment. Then, the troops were armed with firearms and cannons as opposed to swords. Some profit was made from selling such equipment, though this went mainly to the United States, where the weapons were made, and not to Japan.

Customers' needs change, thought this often gets overlooked by many companies, even though it may lead to a major shift in market opportunities. In his book *Value Migration*, Adrian J. Slywotzky describes his strategic prevention model. With application of this model, enterprises will be able to develop their preventive new business solutions in time.

The economic opportunities of today are very much influenced by globalization and technical developments. They are additionally influenced, however, by both the relaxing of economic regulations (deregulation) that brings enterprises in a dominant position back to operating within a competitive framework and the various trends of nationalization versus privatization.

The moving spirit is humanity itself, which becomes the most important element in the value-migration process. The moving force behind human development always means looking for new and better solutions to problems. They call the twenty-first century the era of individualism. In addition, we can say that it is the era of diversity, and one in which people are showing an increased interest in more differentiated ways of operating.

In the seventies, only one channel broadcast the annually organized dance music festival. The participants mostly remained the same from year to year, with only a few new faces appearing, so the singers discovered and noted in the seventies were easily identifiable. Their careers could be followed even by those who weren't that interested in the topic. Nowadays, television channels are constantly competing with each other, trying to find newer and newer faces. Because of the annual inundation of new stars, percentage-wise, a lot fewer musicians are able to keep afloat, hold people's interest, and remain in the limelight permanently compared to previous years. Viewers are told to seek diversity rather than appreciate what's old. As everywhere else, the rules of consumer society predominate here.

All these influences bring about significant market changes, while market segments become obsolete and new opportunities open up. The migration of values influences the profitability and outlook of companies. It is the duty of managers to make a mapping of such trends in time—simply because they carry risks but, at the same time, opportunities too. Those who notice trends first will be the most successful in exploiting the latest opportunities.

The increased use of the Internet has opened up a myriad of new business possibilities. There are several different types of online social-networking services (like Facebook), but only the pioneering ones will gain notable success, and those who copy them will lag behind. Another example is e-commerce. It is worth taking a look at *The Long Tail* by Chris Anderson to understand the extraordinary and important features of the world established via digital technology. We are talking about several economies, not just a single one. Sensible rule-making and the secret of successful business lies in understanding the operation of these economies. Anderson describes accurately and clearly the area and its importance lying behind the peak of the curve.

The migration of values speeds up increased market competition. The solution is concentrating on customers and customer needs. Jack Welch, the chairman of GE, said to his employees, "Companies can't give job security—only customers can."

Values change, but our customers (might) stay if we satisfy their needs.

3.11 WHAT THE CATASTROPHE OF THE *TITANIC* WARNS US ABOUT

The key is not to predict the future, but to be prepared for it.
—Pericles

Five days after leaving Southampton on April 10, 1912, the *Titanic* passenger ocean liner, on both its maiden and last voyage, collided with an iceberg and sank. Although no official passenger list is known to be in existence, an estimated 1,503 people died in the catastrophe; a mere 705 survived it.

It seemed as though the designers, tour operators, and program organizers for the *Titanic* had thought of everything that might provide a comfortable mode of living on the ship—at least in a first-class compartment. The length of the *Titanic* was 269.1 meters. The ship burned 825 tons of coal daily but only emitted smoke from three chimneys. The fourth chimney was ornamental. The ship had 885 crew members, out of which only 66 were sailors. Among them, there were many engineers and stokers and 494 staff serving customer needs. The salary of the captain, Edward Smith, was $170 (amounting to $12,300 today) while the worst-earning members of the crew, the chambermaids, were only getting three pounds, ten shillings per month (equivalent to about $410 today).

I collected from some articles a few interesting details of the last hours:

- On the evening of April 14, 1912, a ship called the *Baltic* noticed an iceberg. Captain Edward John Smith received the report. The captain handed the report over to Joseph Bruce Ismay, a senior officer of the White Star Line. According to some reports, Ismay wanted to break the record for crossing the Atlantic, and he pressured the captain into carrying on at full speed. The Titanic was doing 22 knots (about 40 kms per hour, or 25 miles per hour) on the icy water.
- Around midnight, a cargo ship called the *Californian* passed three icebergs located at 42°03′ N and 49°09′ W. When informed about these, the captain changed the course of the *Titanic*. He headed slightly more southward—as opposed to their original plans—because of the danger of pack ice.
- Later that evening, local time, a ship called the *Mesaba* reported an iceberg in the *Titanic*'s path. There is no evidence that the message ever made it to Captain Smith. The operator, Jack Phillips, was so busy in those minutes sending all the messages that had amassed during the day that he put aside the warning from the *Mesaba*.

Let's stop here for a few moments and talk about business, rather than sailing or the *Titanic*. The source of the information a manager receives and what that information is are important details. It is even more important whether he receives it in time or not. During my working life, I have encountered situations when at the time of preparing for a business decision, I received a dollar and cent (Hungarian Forint and Fillér) accurate prediction from financial analysts; indeed, they even argued about the most suitable amount of cents, which was a total waste of time. The calculations were partially based only on assumptions—we are talking about millions of dollars, so a few hundred dollars' difference was acceptable to me. A manager should well balance the different viewpoints and make the decision whatever the experts' opinions. As F. D. Roosevelt said, "There are as many opinions as there are experts."

There were such decision-making situations, too, when production and marketing were arguing about inventory. Marketing wanted a larger inventory, saying that if they got more orders than anticipated they'd have something to fall back on, while production, referring to cost-effectiveness, only wanted to produce goods according to projections. They were debating whether it should be 10,735 or 5,421. The traders calculated on the basis of the larger number, according to projections, and the production planners did so according to the trend with order run-ups. Since both were based on logical assumptions, we finally agreed on a 7,000-piece inventory. A few hundred pieces fitted smoothly into the dispersion, one predictable from its reliability.

Obviously, planning, accurate calculation, and market information are all factors that have to be taken into account, for changes have to be constantly monitored and kept track of. Nevertheless, a manager should always note the accuracy and credibility of information; besides the estimates, he shouldn't ignore his own experience, and all efforts must be made so that if a business factor changes, he is able to react swiftly and according to the new circumstances.

Who knows what would have happened if Captain Smith, after attending the dinner party of the first-class passengers on April 14 and then returning to the bridge to talk to Charles Lightoller, second officer, about icebergs and the clear weather, hadn't gone to lie down half an hour later but had remained on the bridge? Or what would have happened if Frederick Fleet and Reginald Lee, standing watch in the crow's nest, had not been looking at the ocean with the naked eye only but with binoculars? How would the story have been altered if there had been more lifeboats, and if there had not been just 1,178 seats in the lifeboats for the more than 2,200 people traveling on the ship?

We could go on, but there is no point. The shipwreck now lies about 3,800 meters deep, at the bottom of the ocean, broken in two. Yet it still warns us managers that we must carefully observe even the safest-looking situations. We need to listen to our intuition and use our experience. We also have to change with changed circumstances, to be able to back out in time in the event of an unexpected turn or if we receive bad news—to be able to take the helm before we hit an iceberg.

We must pay attention to the details, but also to their reliability and decide!

3.12 WHAT NOW?

> *In order to gain an advantage, it's more*
> *beneficial if you attack first.*
> *—Bruce Pandolfini*

I went to Murano a few years ago because I was interested in seeing what has become of the reputable glass manufacturing center of the sixteenth century. Murano is located a kilometer and a half northeast of Venice. I looked up on the Internet what was worth knowing about this city. I found the following description on Wikipedia (http://hu.wikipedia.org/wiki/Murano):

> Murano was built on five islands, and its own "Canal Grande" divides the city into two, approximately in the middle. Its bridge is called the Ponte Vivarini, which was named after the 15th century local family of artists. The island, administratively a part of Venice, has 5,600 inhabitants.
>
> The tradition of glass-making in the Venetian lagoons and the surrounding land dates back all the way to Roman times. After the fall of Constantinople (1204), Venice

became dominant in the exporting of various luxury goods, such as high quality glassware, in the Mediterranean region.

Medieval and modern glass production, however, only began on the islands of Murano with the eviction of the Venetian glass-blowing manufacturers in 1291. In the 16th century, the heyday of Murano glass, there were 37 glass-making factories on the island, with its 30,000 inhabitants. Glass, at that time, was one of a few articles of export from Venice. Since the intricacies of the craft were strictly guarded, glass-blowing masters weren't allowed to leave the Republic of Venice. Those glass-blowing masters who gave the secret of glass manufacturing away to strangers got the death penalty. ...

The 1797 French occupation meant the end of the Republic and the glass industry. France in 1814 handed Venice over to the Habsburg Empire, which supported and aimed to reinforce the Imperial Bohemian glass industry; so it imposed heavy taxes in Murano on imports of essential raw materials. In 1800, there were still 24 glass factories operating on the island; 20 years later, however, only 13 remained, out of which a mere five were blowing glass. ...

During the hundred years between 1860 and 1960, Murano companies became world famous once again by producing decorative glass ornaments. A few hundred years after its primacy, Murano had taken the lead again! Murano still exports its traditional products—mirrors and other glassware—but has also introduced a new range of consumer goods, such as faucet handles, glass lamp shades and electric chandeliers. With the increase in tourist traffic, there has been a growing demand for glass jewellery and souvenirs as well.

I visited Murano as a tourist, though the history of glass manufacturing had already got me thinking. Successful decades had been followed by a decline, and then there was more success, and after that more hard times. It reminds me of the fur of a tiger—now black, now orange, the stripes following each other. Now Murano is back at the top again, using many years of experience but with a new basis of innovative, creative, and contemporary articles rather than outdated ones.

If, in the long run, we examine the influences of a business force field on a company, then, according to Harvard Business School professor Michael Porter, the following five elements define an enterprise's competitive position:

1. The aggressiveness of competitors
2. The efficiency of suppliers
3. The commitment of business partners
4. Opportunities for emerging competitors
5. The introduction of new technologies that can enable multisite manufacturing of a product

I could mention an additional, sixth element or item, namely changes in fashion and taste, for which Murano serves as a good example. Murano masters closely guarded their production secrets to the point where people were given the death penalty for giving them away, but in spite of this, as time passed by, the secret did manage to leak out and make it to the hands of strangers. This was one of the reasons for the city's decline after flourishing the first time around. The second ascent, in the direction of new fashion and consumer demand, was due to making the right move at the right time. This led to a regaining of competitive position once again.

When managing a company, take into consideration the effect of the force field, warn Shoji Shiba and David Walden in their book *Breakthrough Management: Principles, Skills, and Patterns or Transformational Leadership*. They differentiate between three periods. The first means creating the grounds for mass-production process-control systems, those that were used in the 1930s and 1940s in the United States and Japan with overwhelming success. At this stage, a company operated according to planned processes, and since there was market under-supply, there was no need for any reconsideration of procedures.

The second period is the time of gradual development, such as the Kaizen model, which was developed in Japan in the 1970s and 1980s. These methods are well known worldwide and are based on several techniques (including Lean Six Sigma). At this stage, companies have to perform well in an increasingly competitive and full marketplace. As a result of the impact of price competition, a demand for cutting production costs appears, and this is exactly the essence and purpose of continuous development. The increasing complexity of economic life, globalization, the constant demands of consumer society for something new, and accelerated technological development mean that neither the laid-down regulations nor the next level, constant development (Kaizen) are sufficient for ensuring a company's cash-generating ability.

The third period of company management is breakthrough development, which was developed from the late nineties in American and Japanese firms; it tries to create a business model for today's challenges. Breakthrough development assumes that the commodity the company produces or the service it provides will become obsolete after a while and that life cycles gradually become shorter. Thus, companies aim at a complete product change rather than just giving the existing one a facelift. Think of the development of the automobile industry or accelerations in product model changes. A few decades ago, one specific model would be available for ten or fifteen years. Nowadays, if a company wants to stay in the race, it launches a new product almost on an annual basis. There are no complete technological changes made; most of the time, it is merely an alteration in the design. Yet every two or three years, you have to come up with something new to maintain consumer interest.

Today's successful companies apply a combination of these three methods. After launching the product and related processes, as long as sales increase, all can be managed on the basis of the principle of continuous improvement. By the time fashions have changed and the market rate is entering a declining phase, a fresh product is ready to be launched, which means that principles of breakthrough development are being endorsed.

Adam and Steven were mechanics. In the early nineties, this profession was still flourishing. They liked their profession. Being neighbors and friends, they often got together on weekends for some DIY and thought about innovations they might come up with. Even everyday objects can be redesigned in a way that is not art for art's sake but gives significantly more to the user. They weren't speculating about such ways of moving, however—they just wanted to create something special.

Generally speaking, the simplest ideas become the most successful ones. One time, Steven arrived late for their weekend DIY, which normally took place in Adam's garage workshop. "I was struggling with that lousy socket again!" said Steven. "I've asked my wife several times not to pull the plug out by the cord, because she will take the whole socket out of the wall. I've had to mend it again!"

Adam was repairing a radio, putting the screws back in their places. "We always argue about that too," he said. "We should send the wives on some training to learn how to pull a plug out!"

They both laughed, but suddenly Adam said, in a serious tone, "Hey, why can't the plug come out by itself?" And a month later the prototype for a socket from which you didn't have to pull the plug was born. They patented their idea, and half a year later found a manufacturer-to-be. They sold their "simple" idea to the electrical products manufacturer Villker Ltd. The firm didn't need much convincing, despite the simplicity of the idea, for it represented a major addition to its product range.

This is a fine example of breakthrough development, even if the initiating of the development didn't occur on purpose.

If you don't innovate, you will lag behind!

3.13 THOSE WHO DON'T THRIVE, DECLINE

The measure of business performance is profit.
—*Peter F. Drucker*

An enterprise has to invest in different resources to produce results. We tend to ignore this essential and self-evident notion if we don't operate our own business. If you are captain of your own ship and run your own business, you can closely observe events with the master's eye. Because of liquidity issues (if for nothing else), we keep an eye on the development of revenue and expenditures. This part of the business is simple math: if revenue is higher than expenses, we grow; if it's lower, we will experience a decline.

But how shall we build a profitable business model? Is there a generally applicable principle in today's complex, global world that can help us plan our business processes independently of the market and the product? In his book *The Art of Profitability*, Adrian Slywotzky describes profit models. If out of these you choose a functional marketing structure suitable for a particular product and market environment, you will be able to draw up an operational business plan.

Not all models are applicable to every market segment, so you must choose the right one. And the most important rule is that every development or new invention must be tested. Reality can always provide aspects that are initially hidden, while well-known ones might also change from time to time.

But what does a model like this look like? Let's consider perhaps the most popular: the pyramid profit model. This model is applicable if the product range has been built up, one product upon the other, like the stages of a pyramid. Roughly the same product should be looked at, though the product's functions, quality, and design expand with an increasing price as you proceed up the stages of the imaginary pyramid.

For example, if we want to buy a paintbrush, we can choose a plastic-handled one with a nylon filament, coming in a few different sizes, or perhaps a wood-handled one with ordinary animal bristles, which comes in more sizes than the plastic-handled ones. Yet we also have an option to buy from a massive range of wood-handled paintbrushes with quality animal bristles.

The plastic one is obviously the cheapest, while the one with the quality animal bristles is the most expensive. Owing to its low price, the best-selling product will be the plastic paintbrush and not the higher-quality, higher-priced one. From a manufacturer's point of view, the low-price, high-volume commodity sits at the base of the pyramid. As we advance up the pyramid, the volume decreases and, in parallel with this, the manufacturing expenses increase.

An even more illustrative example might be the Vertu model from the world of mobile phones, especially the one decorated with Swarovski crystals. Only a few thousand were made. In contrast with this, the company also annually produces tens of millions of models that can be obtained for a few dollars—and a new contract, of course!

It is important, therefore, to choose the right business model when we draw up our business plan. If we plan well, sales volume forecasts will be reliable too; if we don't, we can make a big mistake that might result in serious liquidity problems.

Hans was commissioned to start up a manufacturing plant for a new line of business at Kruger Ltd. The firm manufactured vehicle components. Because of business connections, they had an opportunity to expand their existing product portfolio with a range of products based on a similar production technology that had promising market prospects. In light of planned rail development projects, the special interface—one similar to that of electrical components produced for buses and trams—offered a significant volume of business. As the outcome of meetings seemed positive, the company made a decision: they would begin manufacturing this product range in a separate and unused hall of an existing plant. Since they expected a large demand for the product, they decided to make use of a fully automated production line. According to their calculations, the high investment cost would be returned within two years, given a five-day-per-week workload in two shifts.

Hans was happy to take the plunge. He loved working on new developments and was always pleased, at the end of project planning, to see the start of production and that the process was working according to plan. The company planned to do the first production tests in June. After six months of hard work, the conveyor belt started rolling on the production line at the planned moment, and by the end of the month, the last bits of fine-tuning were complete. Manufacturing commenced in July. Hans was then given a new project to work on, and he lived abroad for two years. The next time he passed by the factory, he was surprised to see that it had closed.

"What's happened?" he asked the plant manager. "This was my favorite project, and we built a wonderful production line."

The plant manager shook his head sadly. "There is nothing wrong with the machinery, yet we were hardly able to keep up a budget to cover depreciation resulting from the massive investment value. We only receive smallish orders, the workload is one week per month, and it looks like there is not going to be any more. Unfortunately, production capacity didn't correlate with demand."

A reliable business plan requires accurate forecasting, so that a Kruger Ltd. kind of trap can be avoided.

> **Promising steps can lead to failure if we act in haste or without sufficient planning.**

3.14 THE AIM IS TO SURVIVE

> *The great thing in this world is not so much where*
> *we stand as in what direction we are moving.*
> —*Oliver Wendell Holmes*

We often face extraordinary tasks. Either the circumstances change or we are simply not satisfied with the productivity of an old operation. What do we do in such situations? Most of the time, we transform, reorganize, or think of a new way to do things—that is, we implement a project.

The science of project management has evolved from the principles of military logistics. The first documentation of project management was created around 1941 for the development of the atom bomb. After its military use, it was gradually introduced into civilian areas as well, such as in relation to architecture and information technology. The applied methods were developed intensively, and people started using them in the form of organizational strategy at the beginning of the nineties under the term *project management*.

In today's globally and sometimes suddenly changing economic circumstances, project management delivers answers exactly where a traditional management technique might fail to do so. Nowadays, one often has to produce results with an organization that has an inconstant composition, may only exist for a limited period of time, and is often complicated and temporary.

A project deals with a well-defined objective. We talk about implementing a project, for instance, when a professional group consisting of a product designer, technologist, quality technician, and manufacturing-process manager is formed to develop a new product, uses resources specifically allocated for this particular job, and has a deadline for completion. However, if the whole company must be transformed, reorganized, or divided up because of the volume and complexity of the task, this can only be done effectively via carefully separated projects having the same objective. Here, we talk about a program. According to Roland Gareis, CEO of Roland Gareis Consulting GmbH Wien and author of *Happy Projects!*, a handbook for project owners, project managers, and managers of the project-oriented company, "A program is an interim organization that has as its objective the implementation of a single, high-complexity, middle or long-term business process."

We talk about individual processes and tasks in a project or program. What was the moral of the depression that started in 2008? For me, it was that we had to find a new way of moving because it was impossible to further increase turnover the old way. New solutions to issues are needed in business life. Project and program management are the means that have been developed for the purpose of finding new ways of operating, especially if one has to adjust to swift changes and ongoing renewal. So we can talk about a project-oriented company when, within a corporate unit, unique processes occur frequently, and they are implemented within the framework of a project or a program.

When a company elevates project- and program orientation into a strategy, it will have to meet certain expectations beyond the extra tasks regarding the implementation of organizational changes and the introduction of operational rules, though this should be considered an opportunity as well. According to Gareis, project-oriented companies can be described in the following terms:

- The company's strategy is management by projects.
- They use projects and programs as interim organizations.
- Project portfolio and project protection are everyday tools of management.
- Business processes are based on the principle of project, program, and project-portfolio management.
- They run a management office.
- A new management paradigm applies that can be specified via teamwork, process orientation, and empowerment of work colleagues.

But what does *project* really mean? What does a model—one that the briefly explained project program and portfolio management, perhaps even the company strategy, is based upon—actually look like? In a traditional interpretation, both the client and the employers come up with an objective. The objective normally covers a product or service to be implemented, available resources, and the expected deadline. As what is going to be implemented is usually unprecedented and none of the existing regulations applies to it, the functional organizational processes of the company cannot be used in the utilization process. Therefore, the most important element in terms of functionality is the formal allocation of power between the project manager and the production managers. The employers delegate the project manager to select the members of the project team, to determine professional competences, to set the necessary time intervals required, and to work out an implementation schedule by observing objectives.

In order to keep the work flowing and to be able to handle and approve changes, the employers and the project manager will hold regular meetings. They could also invite decision-makers or highly professionally competent group members who may be influential regarding the project to such meetings. After completion of the project, the project's organization ceases to exist. A new project presupposes the establishment of a new project organization, which doesn't however mean that members of a previous one cannot become involved once again.

One is able to see that organizational development can be a risky business. Personal conflicts of interest might arise among team members, or the project manager and the production manager might start competing with each other. Yet because of the uniqueness of the task and the goal, projects generally become successful.

Being competent and having the right expertise as well as having the ability to organize a project well may also come in handy elsewhere—for example, when organizing a wedding. The employers are the parents of the bride and the groom; they express their expectations, allocate financial resources, and lay down the time framework. The project manager is the organizer of the event, who implements everything according to the parents' instructions.

At times, in out-of-the-ordinary cases, one has to resort to coming up with extreme solutions to problems, but at the end of the day, this is just project management too. My great grandmother told me a story that serves as a good example of this.

She lived through the torment of the Second World War as an adult in a small town that had a multinational population by the Hungarian border. There were Hungarian, Serbian, Romanian, German, and perhaps even more nationalities living on her street. The war was coming to an end, and the civilians who had stayed at home had never seen each other as enemies either before or during the course of the war. Starvation and suffering made them ever more interdependent.

There was a spacious cellar underneath the house across the street, and the Serbian man who lived there often gave shelter to his neighbors during bombings. As the front line was closing in, there was more to fear than bombs. When the troops—Romanian, German, Hungarian, Russian, whoever—were moving about, they carried out regular searches for deserters and enemies. A solution had to be found; the aim was to survive.

A lot of people put their heads together and came up with the idea that those who understood the soldiers' mother tongue would speak to them. The Serbian cellar-owner assigned a role to each and every one of them: he told them what to say, who the representatives would be, and how the rest should "mumble along." He proved to be a good project manager, even though he wasn't aware of it and had never studied to be one, but their lives were at stake. They even organized spying so that they knew in advance which country's soldiers would be arriving next.

When the Russians arrived, the Serbian came up from the cellar. While the others quietly retreated to the cellar or came up with the few Russian words they had been taught, he conversed with the soldiers in Serbian and Russian. When the Germans came, the German neighbor convinced them that there were only other Germans down there, no other nationalities whatsoever. They used the same strategy when the Romanians came, and so on. And if the soldiers happened to be overly grumpy or morose, there were always a few bottles of pálinka (a strong, alcoholic fruit-based spirit) reserved for this particular purpose, which seemed to do the trick of calming them down each and every time. The team survived, since its members had organized and implemented everything possible for this unique situation in such a way that they attained their goal: surviving the war.

> **Change if necessary, look for new solutions if things don't work out, but never give up.**

3.15 GUEST STORY

A Creative Mind's Thoughts about Success
Sándor Román
Merited Artist
Creative Director Experidance Production

What will help you stand out from the crowd?

We can only give a guiding answer to this in retrospect. To make a forecast is impossible. There are too many alternatives demanding improvised decision-making at the beginning of the journey, and if we don't choose the most optimal, the result will be open to question, and it may change. There are no one-best-way recipes working in all conditions, so that we might start new ventures from the comfort of an armchair. I cannot come up with one either—indeed, it will not be easy to leave a mark behind us after our final departure.

I confess that I personally have never wanted to become successful. I only wanted to create something unique and unrepeatable, something that is not only valued by me but also by the most important witness or "control point" in the theater: the *spectator*! If I seem successful from the outside, it can only be because I have managed to partially implement the big plan with few hiccups so far. I say "so far" because I'm only about halfway there. For those who are just starting out, I might look as if I'm ready; but from my point of view, I'm nowhere near yet.

It never ends, it's never complete, I never feel that I've done it, that I've finished. There is an unquenchable fire inside me, a demand to improve, for creation, and a constant doubt that spurs me to be astute enough and always ask myself: Am I going in the right direction? Is the path that I have taken the true one? Well, posterity will decide! I can only write down the keystone of my story, according to my own opinion and assessment scale. And you should embed this inside yourself. But don't copy it! If you simply copy it, it won't be yours. Let's begin!

The Start

When I remember my departure point, when objectives began to seep into my purposeless teenage days, undetected, then and there, by me—at that point, probably the main foundation upon which all other virtues could be built was a faith given by God. I'm not talking about a religious trance here, but about an inner strength that, in the vast majority of cases, first shows itself in childhood—that inner confidence that provides endurance and strength during the difficult parts of one's journey. Because there have been and there are still to be plenty of challenging moments, for sure.

László Károlyi

School Years

A uniform set of character traits that elevate and sort out cannot only be measured by grades or school marks; the figures on their own are not believable measures of value. Obstacles will constantly appear on your path—and if you cannot overcome them with a lot of improvisation, perseverance, diligence, professional competence, and knowledge, your personal story will end at that point. I meet a countless number of graduates, young people with excellent grades, who cannot put into practice what they have learned at school and are puzzled over the fact that they are unsuccessful.

Love Your Profession

Theory and practice are two different things. So if we really want to understand the world—the sector where we would like to belong to in the long run—we have to start getting to know the true face of reality during our school years. Unfortunately, many people use the period of gaining knowledge as a sort of playing for time. This is wrong. They pile up papers and don't really get involved in anything (plus they don't even get to know themselves)! Mum and Dad tell us what to become because we haven't got the faintest clue, and we comfortably drift along with the ideas of others. But what do *we* want from life? If, after having read this book, you still haven't got any idea, the bad news is that this book will not be able to provide you with an answer either.

We have to provide the answer ourselves, to find it deep within us. When the compulsory school years are over, we need to ask ourselves: why do I want to keep playing for time? To experience the beauty of gaining specialized knowledge, to fully develop and become the best in our chosen profession, or simply to let time pass and, in the meantime, hope to find out what to do next? We cannot do it without conceptions and goals.

Aim to be the best: every day is a competition in almost all walks of life. People hungry for success are inspired by competition. Nonetheless, if you still feel frightened by this and a weight is sitting on your shoulders, you absolutely have to desire change, to overcome your fears. Hesitation and inner doubts about your competitive abilities will draw energy away from your confident development and will make you drop behind.

With reference to my introductory thoughts, confidence and self-doubt can coexist, as the secret lies in the proportions. Neither conceit nor defeatism leads to success. To build our future, it is necessary to set off with an ambition to become the best, but at the same time we need to take what our fate may bring with adequate humility about our life and profession. Nothing happens by accident! Coincidences do not exist; perhaps we just don't understand at one time why something happens to us in a certain way. The enlightenment will happen sooner or later if we keep evaluating within ourselves, if we regularly think things over again and again and keep the processes under control.

We all have *something to learn* from one another. We often get angry at conditions hindering us, which are normally operated and controlled by our fellow citizens from the background. Envy and professional jealousy appear in our everyday lives and try to influence the way we relate to our environment and our future vision. Don't make war—rather, display an interest! We shouldn't let negative environmental factors influence us and steer in the wrong direction, disturbing the positive picture of our own selves that we have, and also our lives. Always be positive, and in order to be able to evaluate correlations, occasionally sit in the other side's seat and examine the whys from the other person's perspective.

Is it indeed true that no one can be a prophet in his own land? In today's Hungarian reality, career conditions are very difficult! The sad fact is that our small country is struggling with such a spiral of negative thinking that it is either unable to process the fact of personal success on the social level or it can only do so with great difficulty. In a country that has been flourishing for generations, they lift a successful individual onto their shoulders and celebrate him, honoring him as an icon; they show him around in the world, giving the country itself a position here too.

In a country that has been unsuccessful for generations, however, successful people distance themselves, detach themselves, conceal and hide, withhold themselves from others (perhaps our elite Olympic athletes are the only exception), all so that the narrow interest groups governing domestic issues—and maintaining false illusions—will never be forced to actually look into the mirror, to face up to and confront themselves and *really* see what is around them. We will have to deal with all this, here in Hungary, for a few more decades, yet we should hang on to our conceptions regardless.

The Fugitive

All indicators are prompting us to move onward, to proceed, stepping beyond the here and now; for there are no more borders, and, given this, we can leave behind—maybe along with the entire country and its occupants—the period of failure that has infiltrated it and their lives. But perhaps we shouldn't choose this path! Looking into the mirror, we should ask ourselves: do we also want to be fugitives? If we don't, then today's Hungary is a really and truly challenging environment for a success-seeking individual. Go for it!

Look for Allies

This is not the story of lone-gun heroes. Although not many of us over-forties exist who have managed to keep our genuine and youthful ambitions, it's a fact that there are still a few of us about. We should aim to get behind our cause as many winners as possible with a similar ambition from a given professional circle. As I say, they are also winners on their own scale, so this attitude is mutually coordinated. This is definitely a thought to keep in mind. Make your voice heard at the relevant professional forums, live a social life, and belong to all the professional bodies that represent such political lobbying forces as can partially influence the future vision of the masses and ourselves, according to our inspirations and what we vote for.

Never Give Up

It is only an original sin committed against ourselves to chase youthful dreams and illusions through a lifetime if we do nothing, or near nothing, to fulfill them. To deceive ourselves, to lie when looking in the mirror, is one of the biggest sins I know. We need to see clearly to achieve success; and we need to know and be able to evaluate our capabilities, limitations, circumstances, and possibilities. And if we don't lose proportion in terms of these crucial principles, then even if there is no guarantee, we will have a chance to succeed. Best of luck to everyone!

With thanks to my friend László Károlyi, who asked me to elaborate on the above, since his suggestions and the processes resulting helped my mental clarity too.

CHAPTER 4

Summer: Sustainable Development

4.1 IF WE DON'T CARE, WHO WILL?

> *The world has enough for everyone's needs,*
> *but not enough for everyone's greed.*
> *—Mahatma Gandhi*

On January 31, 2000, the Aurul—a Romanian-Australian mining venture—polluted the River Szamos and the River Tisza on the catchment area of the upper part of the Szamos with cyanide and heavy metals. This caused an ecological catastrophe on the Tisza. Huge carp were pitchforked out onto containers. The destruction of fish was shocking. In the researchers' estimation, altogether there were 1,241 tons of carcass.

Traveling further away in space, but nearer in time, we might remember April 21, 2010, when in the Gulf of Mexico the oil rig Deepwater Horizon caught fire and, at the deepwater stage, oil began leaking into the water. The widespread pollution approached the coastline. Probably it still hasn't been estimated totally how great a catastrophe this was for flora and fauna. These events are less of a deterrent when merely seen as news than if one is actually there, on the spot.

Many times we just talk about sustainable development, and chasing profit and thoughtless consumption overwrites this concept. Unfortunately, its importance is not considered even when some tragedy occurs. Companies should be working everywhere in the world in such a way that sustainable development can gain content and meaning in practice. They should only be allowed to operate so that they satisfy people's needs but don't jeopardize the chance of future generations to satisfy *their* needs, too. There are a lot of green "thermometers" and manifold sustainable business reports, yet they bear little relevance when having to take on board other issues—economics-based ones—in connection with decision-making. It would be important to highlight a business concept that takes into account in its manufacturing as well as during planning of services that the produced materials and byproducts will not be harmful to people's health or the environment's and that they be can endlessly reused.

There is a wise Native American saying: "We do not inherit the earth from our ancestors—we borrow it from our children." Many scholars think that we will eventually have nothing to give to our grandchildren because of the human impact on the environment. Numerous reports and opinions have tried to raise people's awareness of the fact that we have started a countdown and we should be doing something to stop it, not just to preserve the Earth but also because of us, ourselves. Perhaps you don't know the very pertinent joke in which two planets are talking.

"You look very bad. Do you have a problem?" asks one planet of the other.

"Yes, torpidity, high temperature ... I have been feeling worse and worse for a while now," answers the planet Earth. "It is called something like 'homo sapiens disease.'"

"Don't worry," replies the first, "a few thousand years and it will be over."

Al Gore's book *An Inconvenient Truth: The Planetary Emergency of Global Warming and What We Can Do About It* gives startling data about the changing state of the Earth. Probably the growing worries also contributed to the birth of the idea, in the fall of 2009, of the "ideology of planetary borders." A *National Geographic* article of July 2012 deals with the work of a scholarly group established after the Copenhagen Climate Change Conference and operating under the aegis of the Stockholm Resilience Centre. This group has determined what might be considered a safe operational framework from the perspective of human development. Their members designated nine fields where uncrossable planetary borders need to be delineated:

1. Climate change
2. Ocean acidification
3. Ozone-layer depletion
4. Intervention in the nitrogen/phosphate cycle (which determines plants' development)
5. Agricultural cultivation of the natural environment
6. Urbanization of the natural environment
7. The extinction of species
8. Accumulation of chemical environmental pollution
9. The rising amount of floating environment-polluting particles in the atmosphere

Since then, the thought of planetary borders has taken root in the world of science. It is repeatedly referred to in the GEO-5, the latest report of the UN Environment Programme regarding the status of the world. The major scientific conference "Planet Under Pressure" held in London recently also brought planetary borders into focus in its message to the Rio+20 environmental summit in June.

But as with any concept, one can find uncertainties in this one, too. Its advocates admit that the current criteria of borders are open to dispute, as our present knowledge is incomplete. The correctness and precision of thresholds may improve when we gain new knowledge, yet it will never be 100 percent. There are also some (dangerous) opinions of this sort: we can cause injury to or harm some boundaries, though without causing irrevocable damage.

All this changes nothing about the fact that a worsening of environmental conditions is absolutely clear-cut. As a private individual I can only defend myself by not minding the outlay of 10 percent more for a brand that is proving its commitment to sustainable development via regular reports. As a manager, I actively participate in efforts to incorporate the concept of sustainable development into our company's values and keep it continually at the center of our attention regarding all of our processes and activity—planning manufactured-product recycling, consciously avoiding the making of environment-harming products, eliminating manufacturing processes that harm the environment via such processes, and constantly reducing negative environmental effects caused by technological procedures. When choosing our suppliers, environmental-protection and sustainable-development factors are also important.

Education in protection of the environment is also a part of the previously outlined statements. We have only one Earth.

Let's preserve the Earth, keeping it livable for our grandchildren.

4.2   WHEN WILL YOU COME, DADDY?

Men have no more time to understand anything. They buy things all ready-made at the shops. But there is no shop anywhere where one can buy friendship, and so men have no friends anymore.
—*Antoine de Saint-Exupéry*

I don't know whether you are familiar with Harry Chapin's song "Cat's in the Cradle." If you don't know it, it is worth listening to—it is a beautiful song, and the lyrics make you think. I recommend this especially to busy managers who have got problems in keeping a balance between work and private life. The lyrics include this passage:

> My son turned ten just the other day.
>
> He said, "Thanks for the ball, Dad, come on let's play.
>
> Can you teach me to throw?" I said "Not today,
>
> I got a lot to do."

It's frightening, isn't it? We think we are on a carousel. We can't quit right now, nor anytime later, either. Otherwise, business will suffer from our absence. We don't realize that the family and the children miss us even more. If a guilty conscience makes an appearance, we create an alibi—we are in a rat race working our fingers to the bone to get money for toys, to go on family holidays, to be able to send kids to college, get a car, and so on. Meanwhile, the years are passing by, and nobody gives us back experiences of common games, long conversations—these are missed opportunities. Quality time is missed first by our children, though later we will be the ones who see it as lacking. Our growing child will be living the same hurried life as ours, the sort he saw and had experienced with us.

We live in an era when everything is changing rapidly. A hundred-year-old traditional order of life is going through an alteration. The widening of choice given by globalization and a prolonging of age is upsetting values. And let's spice up all of this with the generations' different attitudes toward life. The role of work is also being redefined. In Western Europe, the work–life balance was defined first in the seventies, when women started to work in a bigger ratio. Nowadays, it is a much more comprehensive issue. For those who are in their sixties today, a forty-hour work week with the same workplace represented a normal career. People in their forties think that after a busy ten-year-long time period they can recharge their batteries with some freely chosen relaxation. The even younger generation simply moves on if they don't like something.

One year ago, a new marketing manager came to the team. He had worked for a few years in Istanbul, but he "fell for" Budapest, so he moved here. We thought that his international experience might bring refreshment to the work of the marketing team. Yves had been working at our company for eight months when he came to my office and put his notice of termination onto my desk. "Budapest did not appeal to me, you know. My partner and I have got used to spending our free evenings on the beach. We've decided to move to Sydney, Australia."

I was surprised at his sudden choice, and I could say only the following "clever" sentence: "Well, Budapest is not Istanbul, that's for sure ..."

A changing life and an abundance of choices can be a source of danger. We are losing the idea of fixed points. Company cultures are also different, so our seeking a balance may be aided or suffer setbacks. If someone is family-oriented, he will hardly be able to manage in a money-oriented company culture, which requires twelve or more working hours a day.

Personal values are needed. To find a balance, one needs to go through objectives and sometimes make difficult choices. The journey is long, and it will take a long time for a manager to figure this out. It is not just the time spent at the firm that is important but time spent with one's family at home. Of course, business success and a stable and effective company are needed, but the owners and comanagers cannot substitute themselves for family members or friends. Those who live only for their firm sooner or later will be lonely.

The manager's only responsibility is not just commitment to the company—he is also responsible for the roses that he has tamed. You remember *The Little Prince* by Antoine de Saint-Exupéry? When saying good-bye, the fox tells him, "And now, here is my secret. A very simple secret: it is only with the heart that one can see rightly. What is essential is invisible to the eye." The little prince repeated this, so he would be sure to remember it. The fox continued: "It is the time you have wasted for your rose that makes your rose so important!" The little prince repeated this, too. "Men have forgotten this truth," said the fox. "But you must not forget it. You become responsible, forever, for what you have tamed."

We have tamed our loved ones, and they have tamed us. We are responsible for them, for sharing with them quality time, for doing lovely things, for a life full of events.

> **One can feel sorry for what has already happened,
> but one need never regret the right decisions made.
> Therefore, ponder first, and decide only afterward.**

4.3 HEALTH AS A BODY FLOW-EXPERIENCE

One gram of precaution is worth more
than a quintal of medicaments.
—Archibald Joseph Cronin

Usually we quote the Roman poet and satirist Juvenalis's words badly. Most of the time, we use his saying in this form: "A healthy mind in a healthy body." Yet he wrote it like this: "You should *pray* for a healthy mind in a healthy body!" (*Orandum est ut sit mens sana in corpore sano!*) Back in those times, the poet worried about the Romans' lifestyle, though his fears would have been well-founded nowadays too. There is much stress, causing sleep problems for many people; and because of our sedentary lives there are ever larger numbers of obese people, and obesity causes disease, including high blood pressure, coronary sclerosis, diabetes, and arteriosclerosis.

We decided at our company that we would not pray for work colleagues to have healthy minds within healthy bodies. Instead, we would attempt to create a complex medical "program" for employees to use to stay in good condition healthwise. In my opinion, both in private life and at work, we achieve more and perform better, and our days go by more appealingly, if we feel good about and in ourselves. Perhaps the English phrase "fit and well" indicates such a purpose best. Therefore, at this point, the employer's and the employee's interests meet. It could be a common aim, and it has to be one! After more conversations, first among top managers and then among a wider circle of employees, the concept was confirmed as acceptable, and we started the program.

We named the health-care package with its several elements the Sunflower program, because of the characteristics of the well-known, beautiful, yellow-petaled plant. The sunflower, for its growth at the time of the developing of its inflorescence, turns in the direction from where it can get the most sunshine, thus the most energy. The flowers follow the path of the sun, thereby ensuring the maximum light dose for maturation and growing. In other words, they try to acquire and use energy as early as possible. We should look after our health and physical fitness in advance like this instead of just rushing to a doctor when we already have a problem. The aim of the program can be summarized as helping the fragile balance of body and mind by establishing a feeling of continuous fitness and wellness.

The Sunflower program contains incentive directions and most liked activities, which partly urge one to move and partly help in the prevention of maladies. Also, it attempts to filter out health risks and even seeks to have a good effect on the family's general health condition. I am not seeking to popularize the elements of the program (which have been compiled well and logically, I think). Rather, I would like to draw your attention to how important the principle is that caused us to start it—and by reference to this principle, you can see how useful the program's utilization might be.

We speak about this theme a lot, yet we do very little, despite the fact that health and welfare influence our whole being and quality of life. Let's look at Maslow's hierarchy of needs. In this system, at the lowest level of the pyramid fundamental physiological needs can be found, such as food and water. On the next levels we can find safety issues, such as appropriate health care; and approaching the top of the pyramid we get additional levels of necessity. At the top level we find self-fulfillment. According to Maslow, the needs indicated at the different levels become an issue only when the needs beneath them have largely been satisfied. Thus, if you have health problems and suffer from physical pain, you will not be interested in belonging to a community or wish to be appreciated or experience self-fulfillment. Nevertheless, as with any model, statements made in relation to Maslow's system can also be argued against, as it does not deal with every phenomenon—for example, the case of an artist or scholar who endures hunger and suffering for a higher goal.

The psychologist Mihály Csíkszentmihályi also makes us think with his flow theory. According to Csíkszentmihályi, the flow experience occurs when you totally immerse yourself in what you are actually doing. You become absolutely outside the influence of external factors—you do not bother with stimuli coming from the outside. You temporarily lose your sense of time and concentrate only on the given task. The phenomenon did not get the name "flow" by accident, since this flowing- or floating-like state comes into existence entirely by itself. It is free from all strain and comes with a pleasant feeling of happiness, and you end up full of energy and with a real sense of achievement. We can foster flow experiences doing several activities, but there are some basic conditions without which they will not happen. A task needs, among other things, the following:

- preparedness
- clear goals
- focusing
- a fusion of action and attention
- concentration
- directness
- immediate and continuous feedback

My conviction is that health is needed for the flow experience. Obviously, intense physical pain or indisposition does not contribute to realization of the flow state. The fit and well status can lead to a flow experience for the individual and, moreover, contribute to the health of the workplace organization. For this, we must do something. As we get older, we need to spend more and more time and energy upon ourselves, our bodies, and our health—and it is worth it. We should try to attain both the mental and the physical flow experience.

Do something to make yourself feel good.

4.4 THE MANAGER AS A SHREWD ORGANIZER

It is really amazing what people can do. The only problem is: they are not aware of what they can do.
—*Milton Ericsson*

All people are familiar with maybe the most-often quoted Shakespearean thought, from *As You Like It*: "All the world's a stage.

And all the men and women merely players: They have their exits and their entrances: And one man in his time plays many parts." During our life, we really do play several roles, including in our private life, at school, and in the workplace. Roles must be changed, and your chances of being successful depend on how quickly and consciously you are able to switch to your new role.

Analyzing the workplace role only, one can actually have several possible roles. One can behave differently with one's supervisor than with a subordinate. Behavior can be different with less influential colleagues than with influential ones. One can be a well-informed courier or a reserved person. It is not easy to reveal the role systems used in the world of work and harmonize them with our personal goals and values. This is mainly because in order to prosper, the company's aims and others' interests also have to be taken into account, since the end does not justify the means.

Let's look at two specific examples. At D-Tech Ltd., the branch managers for two different products were asked to optimize processes, as there were several activities being done in tandem in the course of manufacturing and storage. The two managers asked for suggestions from others and also from the head storekeeper regarding how they could harmonize the tasks overseen by them. One of them concentrated on the task and had discussions only in connection with this. The other branch manager liked to flaunt the role of well-informed man, even if he was not. During work, there were a lot of idle periods in which people spoke about unnecessary topics, in the course of which he developed his well-informed reputation with unfounded statements. These conversations caused misunderstandings, and the idea started to spread that the storage activity would be outsourced and thus the head storekeeper position would be terminated.

This ended up with the head storekeeper, instead of cooperating constructively, hindering the work. He had disputes with people at every turn and vetoed all ideas. The two branch managers could not handle the task. Their suggestions only partly improved the operational process, and they were unable to present reasonable ideas regarding storage to the management.

Following a short investigation, the cause for this came out. When the head storekeeper had calmed down concerning his own position and everything was made clear that there would be no outsourcing or dismissals, he immediately found his role again and managed to work together with the product branch managers. The three managers were able to cooperate effectively from the time it was seen that this was not against the company's aims—and because things were not contrary to their personal interests. Therefore, results depend to a great extent on the roles we play at the workplace, which largely depend on our interests.

At another company, I participated in team-building training, which was held in the format of coffeehouse conversations. One topic was about the manager's most important tasks. There were a lot of interesting thoughts here. Finally, we made a selection and put them in some order. The fifty participants had chosen the following five tasks:

1. Decision
2. Resource management
3. Taking responsibility
4. Credibility
5. Competence

In this list, under "resource management," we mean that the manager has to determine the resources needed to attain goals, and then he has to organize it all into a procedure by assigning priorities. The employee—the human resource—is the most important resource, and his or her efficient organization is the most difficult factor.

What is the lesson from this? The following: a manager must be an excellent organizer who sees the dramaturgical tasks, knows something about amplification and lighting, and involves himself with the tasks of the producer and even the choreographer. Of course, he needs a professional for every role, yet he has to understand and know his subordinates so as to take their personal interests into consideration before assigning the relevant tasks to the performers.

It is not enough to put on a production well just once. Ventures compete, and something always changes. That is why it is important for the manager to make a good diagnosis of the situation, to determine new requirements, and if necessary, to make use of organizational instructions, putting these into processes before they take a possible turn in the wrong direction. If things go well, applause is inevitable, as in the theater. Goals are attained, and the joy of common success gives new energy to team members.

> **Pay attention to your team, to people's interests, and to the opposition. Create harmony and have many happy days.**

4.5   EMOTIONAL INTELLIGENCE

I know that too much is harmful, even of the good,
whatever you do. Either you drink too much or eat too
much. But if your interest has gone, why blame yesterday?
Instead, have yourself another great day in advance.
—*Ferenc Demjén*

In the future, intellectual excellence and knowledge will not be enough to gain success. You will need other skills for your survival in a changing labor market. Inner characteristics—such as flexibility, initiative, skill, optimism, and conformity—will have a bigger emphasis. Employers would like to find good specialists and motivated employees. In connection with how they might be found precisely, Daniel Goleman began his research. He sums up the results in his work *Emotional Intelligence*, first published in 1995, which unexpectedly became a best seller.

Goleman, who did research with several companies, examined the relationship between intellectual knowledge, professional practice, and emotional intelligence. He considered employers' expectations, communication skills, adaptation to changes, self-confidence, cooperation, conflict management, and perception. On the basis of these, he determined emotional competencies by which persons might be classified. In Goleman's interpretation, emotional intelligence does not mean that we are kind to others or express our feelings and emotions; rather, that one is able to show one's feelings adequately, is open-minded, can accept emphatic feelings, and can work well with others.

On the basis of tests, intelligence (IQ) is responsible for 25 percent of work performance. Goleman concluded that a larger part, 75 percent, is due to emotional intelligence (EQ). But what can we put into this category? We have already mentioned the empathetic way of showing emotions, yet self-management or a healthy lifestyle is also an important part of this. Goleman connects emotional intelligence to these five fields:

1. Self-recognition
2. Self-control
3. Motivation
4. Solidarity
5. Social sensibility

It can be clearly seen that these are determining factors both in the workplace and in one's private life. All this highlights the importance of acting with consideration in our private life too, for it is hardly imaginable that someone will use elements of emotional intelligence excellently at his workplace but be unable to manage to in his or her private life (or vice versa).

In my opinion, it is important to have stable inner values, as on the basis of this we can set healthy boundaries, such as seeing in which situations we might say yes or no. We can bring all this about if we are able to rule over and manage our emotional life. This way, we will be able to utilize our feelings to realize certain goals. Furthermore, emotional consciousness will help us stick to decisions and goals even if sometimes this is accompanied by difficulties and frustration.

A constructive attitude to another person is an empathetic ability, meaning we can recognize others' motivations, moods, psychological type, temperament, and aspirations. Understanding other people, accepting (though not necessarily agreeing with) their inner world, and managing our own emotions—these things significantly improve our ability and skill to create connections. Making and managing connections consists of this: you are able to pay attention to others' feelings on the basis of your emotional consciousness and react appropriately to them. Reacting appropriately means that you react neither disinterestedly nor in an over-the-top way to an issue. By controlling your emotions, you can pay more attention to what the other person is saying and how he or she reacts.

High emotional consciousness enables us to control our changing emotions, so that we avoid sudden, thoughtless reactions. The biggest advantage in this is that we can divide those who are really "for" us from those who are not "for" us, with the latter not involving something really directed against us per se but as a consequence of that particular person's existing emotional state. On the basis of these factors, we can control our own emotions, and our reactions will be more rational. For example, if a work colleague has had a dispute with his supervisor and so enters angrily into the office and soon afterward shouts at us without apparent reason, this is not aimed at us but refers to our colleague's existing emotional state. A person with a high level of emotional intelligence can manage his emotions and does not exaggerate the situation but withdraws into himself to clarify the situation for himself with a clear mind.

The Swiss company group had sister companies in more than twenty countries. Annual settlement of results and approval of plans for the following year took place at an annual budget meeting at the end of each year. Ljubo had been directing the Ukrainian sister company for years. He knew the rules of the company group and had done several budget (approval of the annual budget) presentations. This year, however, the company had come up with a more cautious plan owing to the worsening economic prospects.

As was his habit, one month before the presentation Ljubo went to the decision-makers dealing with the budget, and they discussed the plans that would be introduced. Experience had indicated that the decision-makers did not like to suddenly have new elements uncovered during a budget presentation, thus the preparation part was important. In this case, it seemed to be successful.

The day of the presentation came rather early that year; it was among the first ones. More employees than usual (managers from various levels) were there on behalf of the company group. While wishing he had been advised, Ljubo did not think much about this, for it could be easily concluded that, owing to the risks caused by the crisis, decisions made would have more emphasis than usual. He began to show the slides, but a few minutes later he was interrupted by the chairman of the board of the company group.

"You didn't take into account the regulations determined in the preparation guide. The concept on which you've based next year's plan is incorrect!" the chairman declared.

Ljubo did not understand this at first, since they had discussed all this a few weeks ago, and everything had been all right. Then he started to explain what, why, and how he had done things. And two grueling hours followed. Finally, the plans were accepted with little modification, although he'd really had to fight for this.

Later, Ljubo analyzed what had happened, with the help of some coaching. He understood that the chairman's comment had not been for him but was about the whole situation. Then, in a budget presentation, anyone whose decisions were valuable to the company was able to take part, so all participants reacted in accordance with the role given by the chairman's status in the hierarchy—ignoring the fact that they did give friendly pieces of advice to Ljubo during preparations. The chairman gave the expectations and rules of the game to the participants; in this way, he was trying to give information to those persons who were to follow him with their presentations. And of course, such an occurrence is also an act, because everyone behaves according to his official position.

If Ljubo had dealt with the situation more suitably, with a milder and gentler negotiating style, the budget could have gone through more successfully. It would not have changed the final result to a major extent, but he would have caused himself much less stress and strain. It is worth developing our emotional intelligence so that we can avoid difficult situations, or at least deal with them in a more efficient and better way.

Get acquainted both with other people and yourself, and you will certainly become more effective.

4.8 DIFFICULT CONVERSATIONS

A journey of a thousand miles begins with a single step.
—*Lao-tzu*

Sooner or later in all of our lives, we will get into a difficult situation in which we will have to make a painful decision or talk about a delicate topic. But which type of conversation is difficult? All those topics that wouldn't, in an ideal world, have to happen. Usually, the first reaction is postponement—one supposes that time will solve things. Something will happen so you will not have to make a difficult decision, and you avoid the difficult conversations. Although we all try to avoid it, in most cases difficult situations are inevitable and unavoidable. If a specific and difficult conversation *must* happen, it is better to get it over with as soon as possible, and with the best results possible.

One result of the fifteen years of research by the Harvard Negotiation Project is a handbook on negotiation techniques, called *Basics of Successful Negotiation*. The aim of the book, which has sold 4 million copies, is to introduce effective communication methods and techniques to make conversations easier. There are materials from which one can learn and make preparations for difficult conversations. As part of this research, the authors Doug Stone, Bruce Patton, and Sheila Heen also had a goal that focused on private communication, and they figured out how to make such communication much more successful and effective.

They examined and processed numerous conversations in order to find out and analyze the most difficult conversational or communicational situations. The research focused on difficult conversations with the goal of elaborating new techniques to solve conflicts and make dialogues between persons easier. That research formed the basis of their book *Difficult Conversations: How to Discuss What Matters Most,* published in 1999. Since you cannot avoid such situations, it is worth recognizing the techniques that you might use most efficiently, ones that have already been applied successfully in dealing with conflicts at several points in the world in order to foster understanding between parties confronting each other and facilitating the realization of a solution.

We can make use of this with difficult conversations at the workplace—for example, when informing employees that they're fired, being transferred, or having their salary reduced. Or, inversely, if we're requesting a raise. Or, in everyday life, if we have to break up with someone, if we have to fight an enemy, or if an issue of racial prejudice arises. According to the authors, *Difficult Conversations* is based on the principle that "in reality, every conversation is in practice three conversations." Alongside the real conversation, there are two others inside ourselves. They are inner conversations, and they refer to how we are living and what the things that we are saying to our conversational partner—and what he or she is saying to us—actually mean. The authors explain that typically, we do not doubt our own statements and do not accept our conversational partner's point of view. It is not just what things mean to us that is important; we need to try to understand the other person as well.

You can find numerous situations and several pieces of advice connected with how to manage them in the book. Based on my experience, the most important ones are the following:

- *Listen to each other.* The way from blaming to cooperation starts with listening. You know your own truth; pay attention to how the other person lives through the situation and try to understand.
- *Don't shout.* A cautious, controlled expression of emotions is more useful. Take a deep breath before you answer. If we

try to repress our emotions, they will appear in some form anyway, so pay attention—to the change of tone of voice, to the body language, or to the facial expression.

- *Pay attention to emotions.* They are at least as important as others' feelings. But we must not mistake the heat of passion for an unambiguous verbal expression of emotion. Don't transform emotions into judging. Generally, it is true that we must not deny our own feelings but we should keep them under control. It's also good to know that everyone can have bad feelings.

- *Do not postpone difficult conversations* if there is no way you can avoid them. Yet it does matter how and when you go about them.

ToolMax Ltd. dealt with producing utensils and specialized machines. Besides the managing director, the two branch managers—Thomas and Tibor—handled "operative issues" for the firm. The managing director dealt with sales, while Thomas and Tibor dealt with organizing and controlling manufacturing processes on the basis of orders.

The managing director had been in the business for twenty years. He had jolted the business through the eighties, and then a rapid development came after the change of regime. First Thomas joined and took over direction of the special machine division. A few years later, the managing director commissioned Tibor to take charge of instrument manufacturing. Starting in the nineties, there was a fifteen-year period of development, but from 2008 on the firm had to confront ever greater difficulties. Orders became scarcer and, finally, because of the economic condition of the firm, a serious downsizing became necessary, in which half of the employees would be affected.

Thomas and Tibor each had his fair share of this unpleasant task, and there were many difficult conversations ahead of them. They had to talk to group leaders and manual workers with whom they had worked for a long time. They had to make hard choices because, though there were no problems with such employees' performance or attitude, there were compelling external factors involved. A good decision could not be made, just a bad one that would hopefully cause less pain. As they considered the effects of downsizing, in talks that dragged on into the night, a list was created.

The next day, Thomas talked with these employees one by one and told them the bad news, but he also informed them about the package they would get when they left the company. These were neither easy conversations nor easy situations, but they had to happen. Thomas paid attention to his ex-colleagues' feelings during each conversation. It was a stressful, though calming, day for him.

Tibor postponed the handover of the dismissal letters to the next day, as he was afraid of starting the difficult conversations. But bad news spreads fast! People heard about the downsizing in the special machine division, and they were anxious. The following morning, Tibor was showing the strain. He called the employees he had to give dismissal notices to one after the other into his office. During the third conversation, one of his employees asked him, "Boss, you knew this yesterday, so why did you put off telling us? Just so that we wouldn't be able to sleep well?" There was a heated debate, even though they had understood each other very well during their work until that point.

Only one person remained on Tibor's list. The man was nearly six feet tall, a team leader who looked like he could be a wrestler or a football player. It was not by accident that Tibor had left him to the end. He was a good specialist but a very impulsive person, and Tibor was afraid of him the most. Tibor thought that having told the others the news, he would have gained some experience in difficult conversations. However, because of his poor timing, he had not gained any experience, merely a headache from the stress.

In the end, he did not take on the group leader but instead asked for the help of the firm's general manager. "I don't dare tell him! Maybe he'll beat me up or smash the office to bits!" he said to his supervisor, tapping his fingers nervously on the table. Tibor had failed to deal with the great pressure, and the badly timed, misconducted, and difficult conversations, disputes, and quarrels had completely broken him.

The firm's manager immediately realized that he could not leave this conversation solely up to Tibor. However, Tibor had to develop in this field, too, for a good manager has to stand his ground even in these types of situations. So they agreed that although the firm's manager would handle the conversation, Tibor must be there, too—and he had to be the one to hand over the dismissal notice.

As it turned out, the conversation was free of intense outbreaks. When the terminated team leader had left, the firm manager said to Tibor, "Please write down for yourself how this conversation was different from those that you have already done. It will be informative."

Lessons learned in difficult situations are necessary for a person to become a good manager.

4.7   I OR WE?

> *Share your knowledge with others—*
> *this is one way to becoming immortal.*
> —*Dalai Lama*

Generally, one doesn't start one's career as a manager. When we first sit in the manager's chair, we happily acknowledge our success, yet after a few minutes of rapture, days and weeks of work follow. I have talked to a lot of my fellow managers both here in Hungary and abroad, and if we discussed delegation, almost everyone found it difficult to do, even though they knew it was important. Unfortunately, there are some who do not deal with this even as time passes; they suffer from a constant lack of time, but when searching for solutions and the word *delegation* appears, I mostly got the following answer: "By the time I explain it, I could have already done it." However, delegation *is* needed, because no matter how good someone's performance is, his capacity is limited. It is not the single person's performance but the whole performance of the team that determines what kind of results you finish the year with.

Adam was employed as a project manager at Will Ltd., and he directed a serious rearrangement project. The project manager is not a hierarchical manager. He works alone on smaller projects, and project team members are usually persons delegated from different areas. There can be more "full-time job" team members when it comes to larger projects. The project leader oversees a team, though not within the framework of his own hierarchy-based organization. The project team is created depending on the tasks; the actual construction predetermines the employees' tasks. Therefore, project management is often a one-man task.

Adam had already done some successful projects. The first was the introduction of a storage barcode reader. His next commission was for optimization of the manufacturing-logistics processes. He was working on an assessment of this project when John, the manager of Will Ltd., called him in for a talk.

"Hello, Adam, take a seat," said John, offering him a chair. "The end of the year is coming, and I thought that we could get your annual performance assessment now, around November."

"Of course," said Adam, "but I have not prepared it yet. I suppose if I have some questions, though, we might return to them."

"Never mind, let's do it in two steps this year! Let's have a preparative and informative meeting today. We are planning different changes at the company, and I would also like to know your opinion in connection with them. By the way, how satisfied are you with your work?" asked John.

Adam pondered this; he was somewhat surprised at the introduced topic, but he never lacked ideas. They talked over how manufacturing and logistics were going and where they might be improved.

All of a sudden, John said, "I am happy that you are interested in this so much; you look through the processes and possibilities. What would you say if you got an opportunity to handle all of it from now on?"

"What are you thinking of, exactly?" asked Adam.

"I thought that I could entrust the production planning and logistics to you. In connection with the company's reorganization, we are going to create a new division, and you have just the right experience for this."

Adam thought this over a little, but finally he chose to undertake the task. They came to an agreement, and after two weeks Adam was assigned to another position. The next three months were spent becoming familiar with the new tasks. For Adam, it was unusual to be in charge of several people, and he had to deal with tasks he had not needed to as project manager, such as troublesome operational work and time-consuming appointments. Indeed, Adam felt that he had somehow taken on too many tasks. He did not delegate much work, though; he didn't trust his subordinates, for he wanted to do absolutely faultless work. He thought it was better if he made the reports and solved problems on his own.

By the middle of the year, however, he had to admit that he had rather missed his goals. In June, after a meeting, his supervisor asked him to stay behind for a few minutes. In these few minutes, he noted that Adam looked tired, and he was worried about the delays in Adam's department. At the end of the conversation, Adam admitted that *he* was the cause of the delays, since he wished to do everything and delegated nothing.

"The task I entrusted you with is a form of teamwork—you can't handle it alone," said John. "You have to delegate some tasks. The results from this will be that your overworking can cease, and you will be able to concentrate on what is most important. But it will be useful for your subordinates, too. The trust will motivate them, and they'll get to know procedures better. Given this, they will be able to do things more effectively."

Adam accepted the advice, and at the end of the year they had already made up the arrears. Yet the biggest benefit for him was that in the afternoons, time remained for family and entertainment, and he did not have to deal with documents brought home from the workplace.

The team and the manager achieve the results together. There can be only partial results when working separately.

4.8   GOALS AND PERFORMANCE

There is no friendship without trust, and there is no trust
without honesty and principles.
—Samuel Johnson

Most people, when asked to draw their company, lay out some kind of organization chart on paper. However, the reputation of companies is not found in their structure but in their competencies. In our changing world, the fact is becoming more and more obvious for company management that competitive advantage can be found in preservation and continual development of intellectual capital. Human knowledge and commitment are pledges of a willingness to attain goals successfully.

The process by which a manager divides up principal goals for different parts of an organization and its workers and determines what each participant needs to do in order to bring about the strategic goals of the company is called *performance management*. According to many people, measuring performance and the measuring methods used are the most important aspects of performance management. But do not forget that goal realization is only in consequence of how motivated employees are, how willing they are to work in a team, and what kind of professional knowledge they have. All this will work well if there is trust between the manager and subordinate.

We introduced performance assessment six years ago. At the preparation discussions, it turned out that many people thought this was an unnecessary trick of sorts—the three-year objectives and a description of the counting method would remain, and the document would simply be renamed. Thus, we created a task force (a team set up for a concrete task) to make a recommendation about the method to be used, and it would be introduced at the management meeting.

On the basis of the recommendation, we instigated three obligatory consultations between supervisor and subordinate, where the person responsible from the HR department could also participate if required. The first meeting, in January, was about presenting of annual goals. Priorities, expected final results, and the conditions needed to attain them would be handed over to the employee. The training would be included in the educational plan too. After a half year, the goal of the second meeting would be an analysis of trends, an assessment of partial results, and determination of possible necessary measures should realization of the given goals be jeopardized. Assessment at the end of the year partly meant an evaluation of annual quantitative and qualitative goals and partly an examination of the person's personal career plan. If there had been a change in functions or new recruits coming during the year, an evaluation meeting would be held in the sixth month of the assignment, in the course of which we looked at the person's integration into functions and tasks (what is in order and what might need to be developed). These meetings built trust and accelerated decision-making.

When we introduced this process, the area managers understood it is more than just speaking about goal-related tasks and values. The employee's personal goals and career plan are emphasized. On the one hand, this is motivating, and on the other, it keeps a person's faith in achieving goals intact. We had a big delay the first year; the meetings were not held on time, as there were always more important things to do. In the second year, managers and employees started to see the program's advantages. Direct communication led to a more effective information flow, more motivated workers, and better results, because people believed in the success of the team and in the team itself. Turnover approached zero, and on "the best workplace" survey, over five years we managed to improve results by almost 50 percent, for an industrial-national second-place position last year.

A tale about mice comes to mind in relation to performance and the power of faith. The mouse Cini and his family lived in the pantry of a hunting lodge. The fussy mouse Mini lived in the nearby corner, alone. It was not the best place in terms of food, for the master of the house came home rarely and stayed little. Now the pantry was filled, and the Cini family had lots of tasty morsels. Sometimes a piece of cheese fell under the table, sometimes a small piece of bread, and these were a major help in the poor times, when the house was empty. In those times, they searched for seeds or something else to gnaw. They got used to this lifestyle, and they did not even think of moving into the village, where, allegedly, all pantries were full and one did not need to wait for the master of the house to come along.

They were now pondering the fact that it was time for the master's visit, because he hadn't been there for about a month. The cold weather had come, snow covered the earth, and it became harder and harder to find seeds.

"What about us? We will starve to death!" lamented Mini.

"Don't frighten my family," answered Cini. "One, Two, Three, line up!" he told the little mice, and they got into a line nicely.

Suddenly, a noise came from outdoors, so the mice instantly fled to the safety of the mouse hole. The master of the house entered, put down his tools and a bucket in which he poured five liters of milk he had got from a neighbor, and started to prepare for some hunting. As it was getting dark, he hurried off.

Slowly everything calmed down. Cini, One, Two, Three, and Mini poked their heads out of the mouse hole, weakened by hunger and the smell of fresh milk. They set out for the milk can, almost as sleepwalkers. They climbed up to the rim of the bucket, and they tried to reach the milk by bending over its rim. They leaned over more and more, until finally they slipped and fell into the milk! There was a big feast and great happiness, however. They lapped up the milk, but then they realized that they were trapped. They had been swimming and thrashing about for more than two hours and now had muscle strain and could hardly move their legs.

"We'll drown!" squeaked Mini, frightened.

"Let's grab each other—we'll save time this way. And let's think, because there must be some kind of solution here," said Cini.

They held on to each other, Cini and the little mice. They also called Mini, but she was frightened and thought that there was no way out. She gave up and slowly sank into the milk.

"Don't look anywhere, One, Two, Three—tread, in unison! This way, we'll have time, alternately, for relaxation," commanded Cini. "We will have the solution in a minute," he said, though he did not know what it might be. "Let's go, One, Two, Three! You will see that the master of the house will get home, he'll pour out the milk, and we will be saved! You just hold on together, according to our plan! Let's go, let's go!"

It was already dawn when they felt firm ground under their little pads. The milk had become butter from the nonstop treading, and the mice climbed from the mound of butter to the rim of the bucket and flopped down onto the floor. They had survived! After a while they were back, relaxing, in the safe mouse hole.

I don't think I can summarize things more pertinently than by this quotation from Sándor Weöres: "Below is the earth, above is the sky, and inside you, the ladder." We can only attain our goals (whether a business objective or a private goal) if we constantly step higher on the ladder rungs of our performance, believing in realization. If we do not believe in realization, we will never reach our goal, and the ladder will collapse.

If we don't believe in our aims, let's reformulate them; for you can be successful only if you do not give up.

4.9   WISE PRESENTATION

What we think, we become.
—Buddha

For those who are often in a situation where they have to express and support concepts or recommendations in front of a large audience, it is important to know how to convey one's message in the most effective way. There are people who are masters at this. I would like to take an admiring look at the lecturing skills of Steve Jobs, who has been written about to a major extent, since he always used original, very visual slides with obvious ease and naturalness. His lecturing style was pleasant and effortless. His presentation was always in perfect harmony with what he said, and he built up trust with his friendly presentation style. His presentations were so well-structured that the audience was willing to fully immerse itself in them. He was an outstanding lecturer. It is worth learning from him, because a presentation can be a question of vital importance.

Think back to your latest challenging presentation that didn't succeed as well as it might have. Perhaps there were hindering circumstances? Would it have succeeded better perhaps if you had automatically known the answers to difficult questions? In my experience, with difficult questions from provocative or hostile listeners, a neutral and nonaggressive answer always proves more effective than showing annoyance or being defensive. At times, in the course of a presentation, it is inevitable that you'll need to answer questions posed by a hostile client or supervisor. Usually these individuals are not led by a desire to have the truth revealed; rather, they are trying to divert your thoughts or make you look unprepared. This happens to even the best lecturers. The main point is not to see fault-finders as enemies. If there is an enemy at all, we need to look for it in ourselves.

Jigoro Kano formulated one of the big secrets of judo in this way, as related by Garr Reynolds in his book *Presentation Zen*: "Victory over the opponent is achieved by giving way to the strength of the opponent, adapting to it and taking advantage of it, turning it in the end to your own advantage." This lesson can be useful for a presentation. From my experience, if we want to make a successful presentation, we have to take care of the following:

- Find out who the listeners will be, to what extent they know the topic, and what kind of feelings they have about it.
- Your presentation must have a well-elaborated content and logical structure but allow you to keep contact with the audience.
- Attention must be maintained, because there is no excuse for causing boredom.
- Do not hold yourself back. If there is passion burning inside you, reveal it!
- The presentation should not be overwhelmed by detail.
- Use a wireless microphone, move the slides forward with a remote control, and move about freely.

Presentations can be divided into two groups from the perspective of audience. The first type of lecture has an educational purpose, while the second is seeking audience approval.

The first, educational type is an information-imparting lecture, one held typically in front of mostly unknown people. The goal is to raise interest and awareness. Here, self-recognition is also important, along with the previously listed presentation strategies. First impressions often determine later reactions. Ann Demarais and Valerie White, the authors of *First Impressions*, wrote their book on the basis of work done and experiences in their consulting firm. It contains useful advice that can help us do our best not just in presentations but in any life situation. The first impression is divided into seven components:

1. Approachability
2. Showing interest
3. The speaking topic
4. Being revealing
5. Dynamics
6. Way of looking
7. Sexual attraction

The authors' point of view is that every time we cross paths with someone else, we will have a mutual effect on each other. We have a chance to transform this effect into something favorable or unfavorable. If this is possible, it is worth grasping this opportunity, and not just in the case of presentations.

If a presentation is for people who are known and the purpose is approval—the second category—"first impression" techniques are effective, though they will not be as great in degree as at the first meeting. In such cases, of the presentation techniques, the presented data is of greatest importance. Also, there is a different mood when one is reporting on good results than when the results are bad.

I have had the experience of a first-year budget presentation at the close of a very difficult financial year. We thought about the figures all day (questions and answers) but did not manage to get a good feeling from them—and thousands of greater or smaller changes needed to be introduced within the annual plan. This was a remarkably bad experience. The following year, there were very good results, and the presentation given for acceptance of the budget was conducted in a pleasant atmosphere. However, many of the presented figures were proportionally similar to the ones presented in previous years, such as the ratio of direct and indirect staff, relative energy consumption, and so on.

"How is it possible that last year, nothing was good, and now everything is in order?" I asked.

Our experienced chairman made this point: "If the results are good, everything can be explained. If they are bad, nothing is explainable."

The point is to perform well at what one has undertaken to do, but don't forget to convince and win over the audience!

When presenting, target both the intelligence and the emotions.

4.10 BEYOND DECISIONS

Diplomacy is nothing else but allowing others to do what we want.
—Daniel Varé

On the one hand, our century is a world of exploding technical development, mobile communication, and the Internet; on the other hand, it is a new world created by the threat of our running out of energy resources. We might also mention the freedom of globalization, which is at the same time a melting pot and a source of conflict for regional–national cultures. We are seeking the compass that will help us keep the direction of our development on the right path.

Some things are not clear, however: Should we focus on short-term or long-term goals? Should we consider unexpected effects? In fact, why do we make certain decisions that influence or motivate us? Are our decisions based on facts, on rational analyses and arguments?

Do they align themselves with our values, or is there a factor that we ignore but which can still be decisive in the outcome of the decision-making process?

According to the psychologist and consultant Dr. Hendrie Weisinger, if we listen to our instincts, we are "sentenced to" success. As a representative of evolutionary psychology, he explains the development of the conscience and intelligence on the basis of the process of natural selection. Our instincts—for example, the survival instinct—are determinants in our decisions. Although researchers argue over its precise definition, evolution itself is proof of their existence. Weisenger introduces six ancient instincts that he believes, when used properly, can help us find a balance between a successful career and a happy private life. They are:

1. Searching for a shelter—to find security
2. Asking for help—to manage our vulnerability
3. Being caring—to be able to pay more attention to others
4. Enticement—to be attractive to others
5. Cooperation—to improve our relationships
6. Curiosity—to stay ahead

Yet individual decisions are made in groups, to achieve common goals. The larger the company, the more people will have to cooperate for the operation to be successful. Motivation is needed for cooperation. Nowadays, we are willing to forget about our instincts, and organizational models are just that: models. It's like an Excel table—one can put anything into the cells, the function does the operation, and we can instantly read the result. But human behavior is influenced by many things. What guarantees are there that estimations made on an Excel sheet will become reality? How can central decisions be implemented efficiently? What makes a manager and management efficient?

There are various answers to this, but the right one is certainly not what a store manager of a North American electronics retailer said in the McKinsey study "Unlocking the Potential of Frontline Managers":

"They told me: we don't pay you to think; we pay you to execute!" We are living in a global world, but not in uniforms—instead, with unified desires and systems. This approach may be effective for a short period of time but it can by no means be sustained for the long term. This study also came to the conclusion that "Companies that succeed in redefining the job of the frontline manager can improve their performance remarkably."

Another McKinsey analysis directly examined the link between management practice and indicators of efficiency. The study summarizes "Measuring and Explaining Management Practices Across Firms and Countries" by Nick Bloom and John van Reenen. It is interesting to see proven what we actually experience in life as well: a given combination of cultural differences and personal decisions can increase or reduce the efficiency of a company. The McKinsey study concludes that managers who run a company by consistently using the following four principles are more efficient:

1. Knowledge of Lean management and implementing it in the course of procedures
2. Definition of KPIs (key performance indicators) relates to the efficiency of such procedures
3. Right target setting and right outcome
4. Incentive to hire, keep, and develop the right people

In my opinion, this means precise knowledge of external–internal processes and manageability, the formation and operation of these processes, and the selection and development of professionals needed for the task. Of course, the devil is always in the details. It's hard to come up with a methodology to measure what the most appropriate goal is or who the most suitable person for this scope of activities would be. All of this suggests that at any organizational level, the efficient manager pays more attention, consciously and instinctively, to how our decisions are made and what is going on inside our heads beyond merely rational considerations. He or she observes and understands the processes and the hidden impulses behind decisions as well.

This is important also because the managerial role has changed. According to management expert Ken Blanchard, "In the past a leader was a boss. Today's leaders must be partners with their people ... they no longer can lead solely based on positional power." So we have to look at everything differently too. And it not only means what Alexander Graham Bell thought: "Before anything else, preparation is the key to success." It is not just professional know-how and external–internal processes that are important, although these do make up the 99 percent of impulse decisions. The remaining 1 percent may be the determining factor when it comes to a well-balanced, even situation—and here, decisions are made on the basis of this 1 percent.

What does this mean exactly? Emotions, instincts, impressions, and experiences all have some influence on our decisions and reactions. Business KPIs operate like traffic lights: they tell us when to stop, to get ready, or to go. Yet we do not just look at the lights, we also look around at what's coming on the road and how far off it is, and then we make our decision. At times, we do not even wait for the green. We also have to see the connections in business and feel what is hidden between the lines; otherwise, the outcome won't always be the one we expect.

We managed to win a weighty, large business project. It happened a few years ago—a green investment with a private German investor. This was a new business partner, but we had already met several times at different business events and had talked about business opportunities in Central Europe. These small conversations may have contributed to positive consideration being given to this investment, but the most important thing is that the investment decision was made. The fact that we knew the project in detail enabled us to make a complex offer, one taking into account local conditions and with very good returns and low operating costs. Our competitive offer appealed to the investors, and we happily announced that we had won the tender. For us, it was a project of high importance, too, for we had now gained a reference point that we didn't have in the region.

When the first order came, however, the local currency suddenly suffered a significant setback. We had anticipated such an event, but not to this extent. First, looking from inland, we thought it meant a liquidity problem, but then we realized that it depended on one's point of view. Looking from abroad, the return on investment became open to question; yet the national currency's volatility and foreseeable, slow weakening was not a surprise. The project was temporarily halted. Then, after two more years, as a happy ending, we delivered the whole project. At the handover, we talked about many things, including the fact that, in the end, it was good that the project had been brought to fruition, as prospects were favorable and there had been implementation difficulties.

The investor told me, "When my golf-mates said, 'Ralf, you have gone mad, everybody is escaping from there, and you just bring in your money—it is like throwing it out of the window,' I didn't think a lot or look at the analyses; I called my financial manager, and I suspended the project."

So analyses and Excel table data are important, but might it be true that this is not the thing determining the decision? If we can identify the determining factor, we are then able to influence it.

When talking about managers, consultant Annette Simmons said, "It is faith that moves mountains, not facts! ... The real impact on others does not end with persuading people to do something. The bottom line is that people should continue where we finished and because they believe in us." As a manager or an everyday person, we both influence others and are influenced by others. After a meeting or a proposal, the next step might be continuation or bringing something to a closure, and the decision not only depends on the topic but also on first impressions, one's way of presentation or self-introduction. A first impression may be the most important effect we have on others. The skill of making a good impression, of influencing somebody positively, can be developed and learned.

The founders of First Impression Inc., Ann Demarais and Valerie White, built a successful enterprise solely to show people how to increase the effectiveness of the first impression they give.

Their book, *First Impressions*, is worth considering. An interesting research finding cited by them has to do with flattery. Apparently, "people like those who flatter them, and they tend to see them as honest, even despite evidence pointing to the contrary." They question false flattery at the workplace for the sake of realizing one's own goals. Yet showing interest in others is important. For Demarais and White, it is a gift. In their opinion, the majority of humans would like to be understood and appreciated by others, and they would like to get attention.

Steve was a business development manager at Marks Plc. He came to the firm nearly five years ago because of restructuring. He achieved great results, and almost every year he went beyond the targets. However, independently of his results, his local boss and a few veterans from top management couldn't handle his way of working—his always questioning, always thinking up new approaches, bringing up new ideas and ways of thinking. This might be the reason why a good friendship was established between him and two of his fellow managers who had come to the firm at the same time as he: Ian, the financial manager, and Robert, the marketing manager. Not only did they often have a common point of view in meetings, they regularly had lunch together.

After a mission abroad, Steve lost the hotel invoice. While administering his expenses, Ian asked, "Didn't you have any costs to reclaim?"

"Yes, I did," said Steve. "Eighty euros, but I lost the hotel invoice, so I shall make a sacrifice of it on our corporate altar," he added with a bitterish laugh.

"Don't be foolish," said Ian. "Write a note about what happened, with the value of the invoice. We can put it through accounts. Don't pay for the firm!"

"Are you sure," said Steve, "that this complies with the rules and it can be given to accounts?"

"Of course, dude," said Ian.

A few months later, Steve was called in by his boss and castigated for claiming back a business-trip cost without an invoice, for this had infringed an internal rule. Later, it turned out that Ian had reported the issue, expecting promotion.

Impressions, emotions, decisions, goals, rules—it's a difficult network of relationships, connections, employees, and managers, yet we can see the right decision and the most suitable way.

Have your own scale of values, trust your intuition, and do everything to attain your goal, and you will be successful.

4.11 A MEETING OF VIRTUAL TEAM MEMBERS

We people are just like nutshells, you know:
if you want to open it at an improper time by force, it's
almost impossible—but when it has grown ripe, you just
have to touch it at a suitable point, and it will open easily.
—Dan Millman

There are hardly any big companies in which there are no virtual working teams. What does this concept mean? The virtual team is a group having common goals and an ability to perform tasks independently of time and space, so cooperation is realized with the help of different info-communication tools. The virtual teams most often utilized make the work of sales, administration, and accountancy within global projects and at call centers more successful.

At the company I manage, several organizational units operate at a regional level, so our employees work in virtual teams of people from several countries, representing different cultures while working toward the same goal on the same project. Information-sharing occurs regularly inside the team. There are conference calls and virtual meetings, regular correspondence, and webinars where one can make presentations online. If there are questions, you can use Skype, e-mail, Sametime, Messenger, or any other cost-free internet telephone system, one crossing continents.

In connection with one of the international marketing projects, representatives from four countries needed to make a decision. The project lasted three years; in the first half year, members spent two or three days together every second week, but afterward they met less frequently. At the beginning, shared work was necessary so that everyone got to know each other and develop communication standards. A hierarchy was formed within the team, and we had gone through the forming and storming phases of team development (the phases of team formation and harmonization). We brought unnecessary correspondence to an end and the "one mind in two bodies" phase began. This is the third phase of creating a team—the performance phase. Although we were now meeting less frequently, everything was going well, and then an agreement between the marketing teams representing the northern and southern countries was needed in connection with a design. Only in this way was it possible to give birth to a uniform, optimized way of operating.

Time passed; there were a lot of conference calls, a lot of correspondence, all in vain, for there was no agreement. Finally, management decided to settle the case within a weeklong common teamwork program. Even though people's views had showed some accord, on Thursday afternoon there was still no agreement, and on Friday the final recommendations would have to be introduced. Everything was together: planned quantity, technical issues, technology, almost everything on the basis of which we could get the final approval. Only the design was missing. It was Thursday, and we did not want to demonstrate failure, but we were tired of the unproductive disputes. So we went to have dinner but left two colleagues behind. We literally locked them in the office, saying, "You can join us only when agreement has been reached concerning the design!"

At half past nine in the evening, the telephone rang: "We would like to come to dinner. Our common point of view and our recommended design has been sent via e-mail." All this would have required many months without personal meetings—that is, with solely virtual consultations.

What is the lesson from this? Many specialists assert that two-directional, open, and sincere communication is indispensable for the effective operation of a virtual team. Moreover, accurate procedures and well-determined, well-defined roles are also important for smooth cooperation. Yet this is not enough, as team members of different nationalities represent distinct national cultures. They have different habits, and they cannot "read" each others' metacommunication. Being thousands of kilometers away from each other, they do not necessarily sense any interdependence—they may miss the social contact. Because of this, we need to pay attention to interactions, team cohesion, social connections, and the continual maintenance of trust and motivation, even though virtual teams might save on costs and travel fares. We should also take into account the time lag, cultural differences, and the fact that personal and physical connections cannot be replaced by anything else.

> **The virtual connection can solve almost anything, except one thing: the need to look into each others' eyes at times.**

4.12 MANAGEMENT STYLES TAILORED TO SPECIFIC PERSONS AND SITUATIONS

There is nothing more unequal than the
equal treatment of unequals.
—Kenneth Blanchard

We are not the same. And we are not just different from each other, we also change a lot during our lives. Most people live in a way that is cut off from the real world until their twenties, at least in European societies. The sweet irresponsibility of childhood, changes in one's hormones as an adolescent, the security of the parents' house—all give impulses to young persons in their twenties to break out, wanting to act differently and freely, aspiring be revolutionaries. We will also search for changes or generate them rather than suffer from them. The world is opening up to us; nowadays, the limits of our possibilities are sky-high.

People in their thirties slowly begin to realize a harsh truth—namely, that time is our biggest treasure. In this period, there are ever more opportunities to build up a career, though new thoughts come to the forefront: sweet burdens, such as a nest, family, new existential necessities. In our forties, everyone seems to be feeling the effects of needing to change, and we think back over our life. It is not by accident that psychologists see the problems and vital questions of people in their forties or fifties as being part of a specially emphasized and specific field.

What really happens in this life stage? In spite of the situation nowadays, with the crisis of values, more people live in families or in a relationship and have an existence where they are able to provide for others. They are more or less at the peak of their career. Despite this, something happens—something psychologists call a "midlife crisis." People start to assess what they have achieved in life, what they have got, what might have been, what they have not brought about, whether things could be compensated for. A closing-time panic can damage a person's career. According to psychologists, our level of happiness can be compared to a "U" shape: we become more and more unhappy while approaching our forties, and then we gradually start to be happy again, says Keith Bender, a professor of economics at the University of Wisconsin-Milwaukee. According to his age pyramid analysis, there is no explanation as yet regarding why we start to grumble in our middle age, yet we can break out of the daily routine.

Lots of people think that their twenties and thirties were disappointing, and they realize they should have been living another way. They end up desiring a more colorful life, and they may just quit their workplace. Self-revision and self-criticism urge us to make some kind of inventory. In the course of this, everyone will find mistakes and missed opportunities, which can cause enormous trauma. What might the solution be? Those who have a sophisticated emotional intelligence probably know themselves quite well and can handle their emotions according to the situation; they can also give themselves encouragement. Self-recognition, self-control, and self-motivation are all needed for someone to hold on to his workplace and family or build up his career further.

There is a solution to the midlife crisis: According to Andrew Oswald, professor of economics at Warwick University, England, a life crisis after reaching the age of forty might be handled by having a sense of safety at one's workplace or, if this is lacking, finding a job where one's satisfaction increases, the salary is higher, the position is better, or there are more challenges. Thus, even in a life crisis, it is worth changing if it makes you happier.

Then come one's fifties and sixties; here, there is less heat, but people can have the same determination to prove they are able to compete with twenty-year-olds. Besides a desire to prove one's qualities, the existential safety of older age has of course become important too. Such people may decide to change their employer/ employee status to an entrepreneur lifestyle, saying, "That was enough of the robotic life!"

Why am I writing all of this? Because, as managers, we have to know our colleagues. To encourage them personally, we have to know their needs, the characteristics of their age-group, and the expectations arising from the values held by the generations. All this is also part of situation-dependent management.

Much management literature is available in Hungary. One unique offering is the management method developed by Kenneth Blanchard, which is summarized in a journal article on situation-dependent management, "Situational Leadership After 25 Years: A Retrospective," in the *Journal of Leadership and Organizational Studies*. What is its point? Treat different people in distinct ways!

A manager directs his company well if he amends his behavior according to the age of the employee and the situation. Situation-dependent management differentiates between four basic management styles:

1. *Direction*—the manager gives concrete orders and strictly monitors the implementation of tasks.
2. *Coaching*—the manager still gives orders and strictly monitors the implementation of tasks, but he also asks for recommendations and supports progress.

3. *Support*—the manager fosters and supports his subordinates' efforts and shares the responsibility of decision-making with them.
4. *Delegation*—the manager hands over responsibility for decision-making and problem-solving to subordinates.

In these four management styles, two behaviors combine themselves in essence: a controlling and a supporting behavior. Controlling behaviors include instruction, monitoring, and surveillance. We clearly tell our subordinates what, where, when, and how they should be doing their job, and then strictly monitor their performance. Supporting behavior includes praise, listening, and fostering. We listen to our subordinates, support and encourage their efforts, and then foster their participation in problem-solving and decision-making.

To be able to apply these styles, you immediately have to develop three skills: flexibility, situation assessment, and adaptation of style in regard to the situation. Blanchard also suggests that there is no management style that is best in every situation. Do I have to decide, therefore, when and which management style I should be using when facing a subordinate? A decision in this case basically depends on two factors: to what extent I can determine that my subordinates have all the skills and experiences needed for the job, and to what extent I can sense their lack of faith or will.

In addition, I need to know what I am able to do, what things my own competencies empower me to do, and how much I am motivated at the time of my own given life stage. All this makes it clear to me that situation-dependent management is about this: there is no fundamental recipe for the management of people. The only truthful solution to such issues is if we, while taking a maximum of competitiveness and strategy into account, behave in a completely unique way with different people.

With management colleagues, I have done situation-dependent management trainings several times, the first being in the mid-nineties. I myself have taken part in similar trainings abroad, in several European countries. I have good news for the Hungarian managers: the professional handicap, the one that we began our business careers with, has slowly vanished. In recent years, I have not seen any differences between the structures of trainings done here at home and abroad in regard to the content of the curriculum.

Always act and direct things according to the situation.

4.13   NO MORE BAD TRAINING!

Those who think that learning is expensive, give ignorance a try!
—*Benjamin Franklin*

Imagine a factory where an error stops the production line. If it is a machine failure, you call in the repairman, and the problem is solved, at least theoretically. But if there is a repeating quality-related problem, the situation is not so simple. The factory technologists may examine causes, but at such a time it is more natural that the technical expert, the shift leader, the person accountable for quality, and other specialists discuss the things to do. Rarely do they ask the skilled employees actually working on the process to help analyze the problem.

You think that there is a more effective method than this, don't you? The problem was occurring in the manufacturing process and not on the planning table, so it is easier to solve there. This is the essence of the method applied by Toyota and other Japanese manufacturers. One basic element of the Toyota method, *genchi genbutsu*, means "go and see how it happened." With this method, the problem is analyzed and assessed in its real location—where the working processes actually happen. Analysis and recommendations will be made only after this has occurred. As those who actually work on the procedure know the problems and causes of possible failure best, they can give the most valuable assistance when it comes to avoiding it.

The father of Japanese work management philosophy, Taiichi Ohno, realized that there was great development potential in process optimization. After the Second World War, Japanese industry was in ruins, while competitors—led by the United States—were already applying mass production in industrial manufacturing, including in the car industry. Toyota made its car industry competitive in a difficult market environment, using minimal resources, starting at almost zero. The company radically reduced losses in the production processes, sought flexibility in manufacturing, and had a focus on the customer. Quality became the number-one priority.

In this highly competitive situation, quality and the availability of products saw significant improvements. If a series having some sort of failing gets onto the market, it may cause significant reductions in sales, not to mention losses due to repair costs. The actual availability of the product has also become important now. Customers will not wait for the product to show up on the market; they will quickly find an alternative to it—a similar product from another manufacturer.

All this played a part in our decision, about twelve years ago, to introduce Lean management into our company. At that time, it was a very new method in Hungary, so we signed a contract with an English consulting company to teach us the Lean principles and implement some referential projects. A major series of training programs began in which many workers were involved. The consulting company had a large number of references, although none of the companies listed were operating in central-eastern Europe.

At the teaching of general principles, everything was in order. Then came the case studies. Among other things, we learned that a loss increasing in the most "sneaky" way is produced by unnecessary storage ("putting aside in the pantry"), as piled-up inventory can easily cause a liquidity problem, owing to rapidly changing needs. We also understood that one should concentrate on the things that represent value for the customer in the course of process optimization. *Muda* is a Japanese term meaning "wastage." Wastage represents things that have no value to the customer and for which he or she is not willing to pay. Next, we switched to specific examples, and we tried to find ways of operating so as to eliminate losses.

The trainers provided recommendations concerning reorganizing and process improvement, and our work colleagues were really surprised at a few of them at the beginning. One of the recommendations was about the maintenance industrial unit. The consultants asked about revising procedures and, if needed, regrouping machines for reasons of effectiveness; such analyses would then need to be repeated regularly every quarter year.

"Might this mean that we will have to move the machines even after half a year in accordance with market needs?" we asked with surprise.

We could not believe our ears when we got a positive answer. "The monitoring of effectiveness is important, but we don't need details—only the result counts, that is, whether the customer got the product at the stated time of delivery, with an appropriate quality, and how much profit was made on the product? It is not necessary to measure the procedure's phases. An economic analysis is of no value to a customer," declared the trainers.

They could not convince the team of this. We were satisfied with most of the program but were skeptical about certain elements of the practical part. The trainers could not justify these viewpoints, which made people more unsure. Nobody questioned the effectiveness of the Lean method, yet we felt that the education module related to practical implementation contained some incorrect approaches.

This was followed by a few more, similarly astonishing recommendations. The result here was that at the management meeting the following weekend, a uniform decision was made that we would continue with the Lean project, but not with these consultants. It was not the Lean principles that were the problem; we had probably not been circumspect enough when choosing the training firm. The next week, we terminated the contract. Owing to the new, special features of the topic, we looked for a training with a framework through which both theoretical and practical knowledge might be acquired. A Chinese proverb summarizes how an effective education might look: "Tell me and I'll forget. Show me and I may remember. Involve me and I'll understand."

Time spent learning also represents a cost. You should not spend your precious time dealing with autotelic information but with pieces that can be utilized from the next day onward. We decided not to sign a contract with another training company; instead, we ourselves set up interdisciplinary teams for the creating of reference places connected to each method. By teaching ourselves and gaining experience by reference projects, we successfully introduced 5S, quality circles, manufacturing island, and other new operational principles. Since then, Lean has been working well in our company. But my motto has remained the same since this case: "No more bad training!" Only effective training makes sense. It is worth noting that not everything coming from the West can be applied well in domestic circumstances.

Learning is an investment in the future. It does matter how much time you devote to it and how.

4.14 THE UNICUM TEAM

Just as a small fire is extinguished by a storm, a large fire is enhanced by it.
Likewise, a weak faith is weakened by a predicament or catastrophe,
while a strong faith is strengthened by them.
—Viktor E. Frankl

A birthday is usually a memorable day in a person's life, particularly those that mark the start of a new decade. On these occasions, we often look back on our life and attempt to learn from our experiences. Then we look forward, trying to see into the future, though it can also happen that we just feel very good. A company anniversary can be a similar event for a workplace community. The older the company is, the stronger the evidence that the skilled people working there are performing well and believe in their skills and in reaching their goals.

We can assess the effectiveness of a company in two respects: according to annual performance and on the basis of the long-term sustainability of such results. Annual performance measures the performance of the collective—revenue, profit, market-share tendency, and manufacturing costs. This is an assessment of a short period of time. The sustainability of the long-term result will characterize the company in the long run, coordinating over five-, ten-, or even fifty-year periods. There are always alterations in the collective of a company, partly owing to natural fluctuations and partly to economic or technological changes. When we examine the long-term results of a company with several decades-long intervals, we can see significant alterations. This is the measure of its sustainable effectiveness. Before this point, one cannot come up with a precise index number, as many components have an influence on results.

In my opinion, among the several influencing factors, the human resource is the key figure in any realization of sustainable effectiveness. First, it depends on how successfully company management can organize the handing down of know-how through company generations; second, it depends on how effectively persons can adapt to changing trends. By a change in generations for a company, I'm referring to team-member changes due to the natural turnover of managers and subordinates. A new manager and new subordinates bring new points of view and, if the company culture helps in any handover of experience, have an effect like a catalyst when mixed with old team members. Its measurement index could be changes in the company revenue as related to the average revenue increase of the industry's top 100.

Starting from a similar logic, some researchers talk about business life cycles. According to this, companies have the same life path as people. They are born, develop, reach their peak, decline, and die. Naturally, with wise and purposeful management, a company (unlike a person) can operate in the middle, having a well-performing life cycle. I quote the founder of the Adizes methodology, Dr. Ichak Adizes: "To live means solving problems continuously. The more complete your life is, the more difficult and complex the problems you need to solve become. The same is true of organizations. In order to manage an organization, you have to solve problems continually. An organization will have no problems only when there are no changes going on inside it. Yet this only happens when the organization is already dead."

In Adizes's model, he compares the business life cycle with the life cycle of living organisms, and he sees it as an analogy. The stages are as follows:

1. The stage of foundation or courtship
2. Development, consideration of possibilities, initiation of realization, infancy
3. Start-up period, when the sales curve starts to rise; the stage of youthful agility
4. Development, adolescence, when there are many conflicts and lack of consequence (the danger here is that the company may regress to the start-up stage or fall victim to having a loss of aim and conflict)
5. Approaching peak sales, profit, and efforts to get results
6. Era of adulthood, a period of stability; the organization is stable, preserving the status quo, yet the company does start to lose out on its flexibility
7. Era of decline (aristocracy), moving away from the customer, beginning to lose its market
8. Early bureaucracy; survival of the individual, a lot of conflicts, domestic quarrels
9. Bureaucracy equals death, the company turns to face inward, becomes isolated from the environment; upper management and operative management divide up

Adizes writes in his book *Corporate Lifecycles: How and Why Corporations Grow and Die and What to Do About It*, "The stages of the business life cycle are predictable and recurring, so if the management knows where the organization is within this life cycle, they can take preventive action in order to avoid problems." Adizes's work confirms that several index-numbers will be suitable for a measurement of the company's long-term, sustainable development, as there are distinct goals for each stage (including cash flow, volume of sales, market share, profit). According to Adizes, company performance is at its peak within the most beautiful part of adulthood.

However you look at it, reaching and living in the most beautiful period of adulthood points to a nice performance and experience. I had the pleasure and the honor twenty years ago of starting work at a company that had just entered into a new stage of its business cycle, one heading into adulthood. I applied for a position advertised by the manager of a state-owned company, yet the foreign representatives of the privatized company's new owner had already decided about my being taken on.

Twenty years seems like a long time. Nowadays, it is rare that one person spends this amount of time with just one company, particularly within the competitive sector. But I saw it as very colorful because, except my last position, I changed my position every two to three years. Although I'd had an employment contract with the Hungarian company all the time, I did numerous foreign projects through which I worked in a lot of European countries and sometimes also on other continents. Our company celebrated its fiftieth anniversary and, as usually happens, such an anniversary generated several media events.

At a press conference, one journalist asked me how long I had been working with the company. He was astonished when I told him twenty years. "Now, it is unique if someone stays at a company for such a long period of time!" the journalist told me. After the conversation, I pondered a lot over this comment. I never thought that I would be *unique*. Then I thought about how many people I had gotten to know in the past twenty years, either just for a handshake or to spend some time together at a meeting to find a solution to some problem, or those with whom I might talk about anything over a glass of wine or after an evening's sports event. There are a few who have now retired or maybe left the company, though this was not so typical. I am working with others at the company even now. Examining this thoroughly, I have concluded that if I am somehow unique, those who have worked years, indeed decades with me at the same company are too. They are all unique as well. As we are a team, this is a unique team.

It crossed my mind that this is reinforced by the company's performance in the most recent decades, on the basis of which we reached the country's top 500 category regarding revenue and results. Our results improved also in an era burdened by the crisis. We gave an excellent performance. The fiftieth year is a special event, for a half-century is evidence that the people working at the company have always found challenges in what they were working on. Moreover, this occurred in a very good company culture, where people hand over their experiences to each other. This entitles us to hope that we can maintain such a performance in the next fifty years, too.

The main thing is that I am not something unique, but that the team is a unique team.

> **Everything is difficult for one, but nothing is impossible for many. —István Széchenyi**

4.15 GUEST STORY

Summer
Szabó György
Former Chairman and CEO
Sanoma Zrt.

It is obvious that one writes about the summer, and I was grateful that the author of the book asked me to write an appreciation of this season. We all wait for the summer; the other seasons are just a transition to the summer. Life is moving toward summer and gives you a sense of it. Yet how untruthful it is: determining the shortness of the most beautiful season in the same way as the others. One has to tolerate nine months of continuous change in order to enjoy the tranquility of just three months.

Summer is the only season in my life in which the months have their own life, have their own personality. In winter, it doesn't matter to me whether it is December, January, or February. The first month of spring is joyful, we can slip out of our stifling coats and scarves; yet April and May do not show any substantial differences. September, October, November are all the same: I have hardworking, dark, familiar, and repetitive days, and I do not see any difference between them.

And what about June, July, and August? Each has its own face!

In June, I still feel the school routine: the beginning of June is full of obligations, yet from the fifteenth the real summer is now here! I have obligations also in the second half of June, but I handle them more easily because they are enlightened by the easing off that will come with the summer.

July is still for work but also a form of waiting—awaiting the "holiday," though I do not like to consider relaxation a holiday (freedom) because it would seem as if I were not doing my job freely, that I was not freely accepting it as a task. What a good word *relaxation* is! It expresses exactly the idea of being somewhere else.

My holiday must always be in August. At this time, I think we are in the middle of summer. I have an illusion of never-ending light, long days, and warm nights. If I went on holiday in July, I would feel that August was not a real summer month; it would be a month that was approaching autumn.

What is the summer really about? About the fact that we become extroverted, we recharge ourselves with the sunshine, we become open to others and become more receptive. The summer is the season of relationships—or, to use a fashionable word, *communication*. Our previously unsaid thoughts and feelings come to the surface, our inhibitions are set free, and we show ourselves to ourselves and to others too.

The summer is about being somewhere else: we feel that we have to leave our everyday environment to recharge our batteries, to experience other cultures and people who live and think differently. It is a contradiction: we have a rest by going away.

What else is the summer about? It is about being amazed at all those things we have done before the summer, and we internalize them. We accept the previous events of our life and reconcile ourselves to previous occurrences. Here, we incorporate the experiences that we have gained in autumn, winter, and spring into our minds and hearts. Without summer, we would have probably forgotten all the experiences of the previous three seasons, as there must be a period of time when we do nothing but feel reassured and work through things. And we have to go away for this: it is interesting that in another place, we can interpret our experiences better than at home. This is the power of distance—looking from the outside, things we have dealt with before seem to be more valuable or, just the opposite, less than important. We get rid of the importance of closeness, thus we achieve better understanding.

If only there was no last day to the summer! But if there was no last summer's day, the autumn could not start, which, in time, leads us to the next summer ...

CONCLUSION

Adventures with thoughts, tasks, possibilities, and tools, beyond and within the borders of management and culture, end here for the pages in this book. But this is not the case in everyday life! This is a process that cannot and must not be stopped. It is not only to have a chance to be successful but also to be worthy men, as advised by Einstein: "Try not to become a man of success, but rather try to become a man of value." As managers, we need sophisticated values. We have to preserve our humanity and trustworthiness within the changes made.

Life is indeed changing continuously. New technologies, global opportunities, and sometimes threats appear. Challenges can only be risen to by active application of creative benchmarking, or "crenchmarking." Creativity has to be developed, and this is also well served by the method of looking around at other fields. In my introduction, I mentioned a quote by Charles Darwin: "It is not the strongest of species that survives, nor the most intelligent, but the one most adaptable to change." This is exactly like competition in the business world: the most creative enterprises will survive. For sure, there are a lot of good benchmarks to consider. But benchmarks are not enough in a global environment; if they are not combined with creativity and innovation, the enterprise will not survive for long, as it will not find the right solution to the changing business environment.

Charles Handy, an Irish author specializing in organizational behavior and management who is ranked among the Thinkers 50, a private list of the most influential living management thinkers, wrote, "Most scientific breakthroughs—for example the theory of relativity—derived from borrowing something from one field of life and applying it as a metaphor in another field." I believe that the stories in this book will help the reader live with open eyes and an open mind. What is important is not only what we see but how we interpret things and how we recognize their essence. New knowledge and new experiences are all catalyzers of creativity, but one also needs them to be able to distinguish utilizable ways of operating from theoretical utopias.

Everything is continuously changing. If we have achieved our aim successfully at the end of a month or a year, life will set new goals for us. This is an interesting way of circulation, a wandering toward our aims, and it favors our self-fulfillment at the workplace and in private life. An appropriate metaphor for this is a part of Sándor Márai's book *Füves könyv: Gyógyító gondolatok* (Herbarium: Healing thoughts), in which he explains that, in reality, we are always on our way or en route somewhere:

> Do you think you have now built yourself a house— and from the proud peaks of your career you can observe the world with satisfaction? Don't you think that you will forever remain a wanderer and everything you do is a wanderer's movement of someone en route somewhere? You are moving among towns, aims, life stages and changes forever, and if you take a rest it is neither more certain nor for any longer than when a wanderer comes to a sudden stop within the shadow of a roadside apple tree for half an hour. Keep this in mind when devising plans. The sense of your journey is not the aim, but the wandering. You are not living in specific situations but are en route.

Adventures among thoughts, tasks, possibilities, and tools will never end; they rotate like the seasons. We live in situations either as a manager or a private individual, but we are always on our way.

PRO MEMORIA

BIBLIOGRAPHY AND REFERENCES

Adizes, Ichak. *Corporate Lifecycles: How and Why Corporations Grow and Die and What to Do About It.* Carpinteria, California: The Adizes Instiute, 1990.

Anderson, Chris. *The Long Tail: Why the Future of Business Is Selling Less of More.* New York: Hyperion, 2008.

———. *Free: The Future of a Radical Price.* New York: Hyperion, 2009.

Ballard, Robert D. *The Discovery of the Titanic.* New York: Warner Books, 1987.

Barrow, Colin, Paul Barrow, and Robert Brown. *The Business Plan Workbook.* 3rd rev. ed. London: Kogan Page Ltd., 1998.

Blanchard, Kenneth H., Drea Zigarmi, and Robert B. Nelson. "Situational Leadership After 25 Years: A Retrospective." *Journal of Leadership and Organizational Studies* 1, no. 1 (November 1993): 21–36. http://jlo.sagepub.com/content/1/1/21.abstract.

Bloom, Nick, Stephen Dorgan, John Dowdy, and John Van Reenen. "Management Practice and Productivity: Why They Matter." *Management Matters,* July 2007. http://cep.lse.ac.uk/management/Management_Practice_and_Productivity.pdf.

Bloom, Nick, and John Van Reenen. "Measuring and Explaining Management Practices Across Firms and Countries." CEP Discussion Paper No 716, Centre for Economic Performance, London School of Economics and Political Science, London, March 2006. http://cep.lse.ac.uk/pubs/download/dp0716.pdf.

Breakthrough Management. http://www.walden-family.com/breakthrough.

Buckingham, Marcus, and Curt Coffman. *First, Break All the Rules: What the World's Greatest Managers Do Differently.* New York: Simon and Schuster, 1999.

Bulgakov, Mikhail. *Mester és Margarita* [*The Master and Margarita*]. Budapest: Európa Kiadó, 2012.

Butler-Bowdon, Tom. *Fifty Psychology Classics.* London: Nicholas Brealey Publishing, 2006.

Buzan, Tony, Tony Dottino, and Richard Israel. *The BrainSmart Leader.* Hampshire: Gower Publishing Ltd., 1999.

Canfield, Jack, and Mark Victor Hansen. *A 3rd Serving of Chicken Soup for the Soul: More Stories to Open the Heart and Rekindle the Spirit.* New York: Open Road Media, 2012.

Center of Leadership Studies. http://www.situational.com.

Charan, Ram. *Leadership in the Era of Economic Uncertainty: Managing in a Downturn.* New York: McGraw-Hill, 2009.

Cheverton, Peter. *How Come You Can't Identify Your Key Customers?: The Essential Guide to Key Account Selection.* London: Kogan Page Ltd., 2002.

Cialdini, Robert B. *Influence: Science and Practice.* 5th ed. Boston: Pearson Education, 2009.

———. *Influence: The Psychology of Persuasion.* rev. ed. New York: Harper Business, 2006.

Collins, James C. *Good to Great: Why Some Companies Make the Leap ... and Others Don't.* New York: HarperBusiness, 2001.

Covey, Stephen R. *The Seven Habits of Highly Effective People.* New York: Simon and Schuster, 1999.

———. *The Eighth Habit: From Effectiveness to Greatness.* New York: Simon and Schuster, 2005.

Cross, Robb, Nitin Nohria, and Andrew Parker. "Six Myths about Informal Networks—and How to Overcome Them." *MIT Sloan Management Review* (Spring 2002).

Davis, Tony, and Richard Pharro. *The Relationship Manager: The Next Generation of Project Management.* Hampshire: Gower Publishing Ltd., 2003.

de Kermadec, Yann. *Innover grace au brevet.* Neuilly-Sur-Seine: Insep Editions, 2001.

Demarais, Ann, and Valerie White. *First Impressions: What You Don't Know About How Others See You.* New York: Bantam Books, 2008.

"Department of Management." LSE Management. http://www.lse.ac.uk/management/home.aspx.

de Saint-Exupéry, Antoine. *The Little Prince*. New York: Harcourt, 2000.

de Smet, Aaron, Monica McGurk, and Marc Vinson. "Unlocking the Potential of Frontline Managers." McKinsey and Company, August 2009. http://www.mckinsey.com/insights/organization/unlocking_the_potential_of_frontline_managers.

Drucker, Peter F. *The Effective Executive: The Definitive Guide to Getting the Right Things Done*. London: Heinemann Professional Publishing, 1985.

Exley, Helen. *Timeless Values*. New York: Exley Publication Ltd., 2002.

Farkas, Charles M., and Philippe De Backer. *Maximum Leadership: the World's Leading CEOs Share Their Five Strategies for Success*. New York: Henry Holt and Company, 1996.

Ferenc, Farkas. *Változásmenedzsment*. Budapest: Akadémia Kiadó Zrt., 2005.

Foster, John Wilson. *The Titanic Complex*. Vancover: Belcouver Press, 1997.

Frame, J. Davidson. *The New Project Management: Tools for an Age of Rapid Change, Complexity, and Other Business Realities*. San Francisco: Jossey-Bass, 2002.

Gábor, Pesthy. "Bölcsen döntöttek a tigrisek." *Origo* (September 4, 2012). Accessed September 21, 2012. http://www.origo.hu/tudomany/20120904-a-nepali-igyekszenek-elkerülni-az-embereket.html (site discontinued).

Gallo, Carmine. *The Presentation Secrets of Steve Jobs: How to Be Insanely Great in Front of Any Audience.* Grand Haven: Brilliance Publishing, 2012.

Goethe, J. W. *The Sorrows of Young Werther.* London: Vintage, 1973.

Goleman, Daniel. *Emotional Intelligence: Why It Can Matter More Than IQ.* New York: Bantam Books, 2005.

Gore, Al. *An Inconvenient Truth: The Planetary Emergency of Global Warming and What We Can Do About It.* New York: Rodale Books, 2006.

Handy, Charles. Quoted in Gondolatok. http:// www.uzleticoach.hu/ elements/gondolatok.swf.

Heider, John. *The Tao of Leadership: Lao Tzu's Tao Te Ching Adapted for a New Age.* Atlanta: Edge 2000 Ltd., 2004.

Herr, Hugh. "The New Bionics That Let Us Run, Climb, and Dance." YouTube. http://www.youtube.com/ watch?v=CDsNZJTWw0w&list=PLOGi5-fAu8bHBh9lg_4t- qcCa8l625Rhg.

Hindle, Tim. "Genchi Genbutsu." *The Economist,* October 13, 2009. http://www.economist.com/node/14299017.

Hirn, Wolfgang. *Herausforderung China: wie der chinesische Aufstieg unser Leben verändert.* Frankfurt am Main: Fischer Taschenbuch Vlg., 2006.

Hoff, Benjamin. *The Tao of Pooh.* New York: E. P. Dutton Inc., 1982.

Horváth, Péter. *Controlling.* Budapest: Közgazdasági és Jogi Kiadó, 1993.

Huxley, Aldous. *Island*. London: Vintage, 2005.

Iacocca, Lee. *Iacocca: An Autobiography*. With William Novak. New York: Bantam Books, 1985.

Jigaro, Kano. quote http://books.google.com/books?id=4VRs CspB080C&printsec=frontcover&dq=presentation+zen&hl= en&sa=X&ei=IyxEVKG9BY6ayASas4II&ved=0CDgQ6AEw AQ#v=onepage&q=kano&f=false.

Kaplan, Robert S., and David P. Norton. *Strategy Maps: Converting Intangible Assets into Tangible Outcomes*. Boston: Harvard Business School Press, 2004.

Karoliny Mártonné et al. *Emberi erőforrás menedzsment kézikönyv*. Budapest: KJK-Kerszöv. Jogi és Üzleti Kiadó Kft., 2004.

Kawasaki, Guy. *Enchantment: The Art of Changing Hearts, Minds, and Actions*. New York: Penguin Group, 2011.

Komócsin, Laura. *Módszertani kézikönyv coachoknak és coachingszemléletű vezetőknek I*. Budapest: Manager Könyvkiadó, 2009.

———. *Módszertani kézikönyv coachoknak és coachingszemléletű vezetőknek II*. Budapest: Manager Könyvkiadó, 2011.

Korda, Michael. *Power!: How to Get It, How to Use It*. New York: Warner Books, 1991.

Kotler, Philip. *Kotler on Marketing: How to Create, Win, and Dominate Markets*. New York: The Free Press, 1999.

Kotler, Philip, and John A. Caslione. *Chaotics: The Business of Managing and Marketing in the Age of Turbulence*. New York: Amacom, 2009.

Kotler, Philip, and Kevin Lane Keller. *Marketing Management.* 12th ed. Boston: Pearson Education, 2006.

Kotter, John. *Our Iceberg Is Melting: Changing and Succeeding Under Any Conditions.* New York: St. Martin's Press, 2006.

Levinson, Jay Conrad. *Guerilla Marketing: Secrets for Making Big Profits from Your Small Business.* Boston: Houghton Mifflin Company, 1984.

Liker, Jeffrey K. *The Toyota Way: Fourteen Management Principles from the World's Greatest Manufacturer.* New York: McGraw Hill, 2004.

Little, Edward, and Ebi Marandi. *Relationship Marketing Management.* Stamford: Cengage Learning EMEA, 2003.

Losey, Mike, Sue Meisinger, and Dave Ulrich, eds. *The Future of Human Resource Management: Sixty-Four Thought Leaders Explore the Critical HR Issues of Today and Tomorrow.* Hoboken, New Jersey: Wiley and Sons, 2005.

MacArthur, Brian. *Penguin Book of Twentieth-Century Speeches.* New York: Penguin Group, 2000.

Machiavelli, Niccoló. *Il Principe.* Translated by Giuseppe Lisio. Firenze: BiblioBazaar, 2009.

Mackay, Harvey B. *Swim with the Sharks Without Being Eaten Alive.* New York: William Morrow Company, 1988.

Máray, Sándor. *Fűves könyv: Gyógyító gondolatok.* Budapest: Helikon Kiadó, 2012.

McCormack, Mark H. *Success Secrets.* New York: HarperBusiness, 1989.

McDonough, William, and Michael Braungart. *Cradle to Cradle: Remaking the Way We Make Things*. New York: North Point Press, 2002.

Mehta, Gita. *Raj*. New York: Random House, 2007.

Mieras, Mark. *Ben ik dat?: wat hersenonderzoek vertel over onszelf*. Amsterdam: Nieuw, 2007.

Molnár, Cs. "Mítoszok és valóság a delfinek intelligenciájáról." *Origo* (August 3, 2007). Accessed August 19, 2012. http://www .origo.hu/tudomany/20070803-delfin-delfinek-intelligencia-kepessegekviselkedes-kommunikacio-eszkozhasznalat-delfinagy-evolucio.html (site discontinued).

Morito, Akio. *Made in Japan*. New York: E. P. Dutton, 1986.

Moss, Geoffrey. *Getting Your Ideas Across: A Handbook to Improve Your Listening, Speaking, Writing and Meeting Skills*. London: Kogan Page Ltd., 1989.

"Murano." *Wikipedia*. http://hu.wikipedia.org/wiki/Murano.

Norbert, Izsáki. "Csomópontosítók." *HVG*, May 23, 2012. http:// hvg.hu/hvgfriss/2012.21/201221_a_halozatelemzes_haszna_csomopontositok.

Pandolfini, Bruce. *Every Move Must Have a Purpose: Strategies from Chess for Business and Life*. New York: Hyperion, 2003.

"Planetáris határok" [Planetary boundaries]. *National Geographic Magyarország*, July 2012. http://www.ng.hu/Fold/2012/07/planetaris_hatarok.

Rad, Parviz F., and Ginger Levin. *Achieving Project Management Success Using Virtual Teams.* Boca Raton: J. Ross Publishing Inc., 2003.

Rajna, Péter. *Fekete bárányok és fehér hollók.* [Black sheep and white ravens]. Budapest: Ad Solutions Kiadó, 2012.

Reynolds, Garr. *Presentation Zen: Simple Ideas on Presentation Design and Delivery.* Boston: Pearson Education, 2008.

Ridderstale, Jonas, and Kjell A. Nordström. *Karaoke Capitalism.* Philadelphia: Trans-Atlantic Publications, 2004.

Seiwert, Lothar. *Die Bären-Strategie: In der Ruhe liegt die Kraft* [Bear Strategy: power through calmness]. München: Wilhem Heyne Verlag, 2005.

Sharma, Robin. *The Leader Who Had No Title: A Modern Fable on Real Success in Business and in Life.* New York: Free Press, 2011.

———. *The Monk Who Sold His Ferrari: A Fable About Fulfilling Your Dreams and Reaching Your Destiny.* New York: HarperBusiness, 2005.

Shiba, Shoji, and David Walden. *Breakthrough Management: Principles, Skills, and Patterns or Transformational Leadership.* New Delhi: Confederation of Indian Industry, 2006.

Slywotzky, Adrian J. *The Art of Profitability.* New York: Warner Books, 2002.

———. *Value Migration: How to Think Several Moves Ahead of the Competition.* Cambridge, Massachusetts: Harvard Business Press, 1996.

Smith, Benson, and Tony Rutigliano. *Discover Your Sales Strengths: How the World's Greatest Salespeople Develop Winning Careers*. New York: Warner Books, 2003.

Smith, Hyrum W. *The Ten Natural Laws of Successful Time and Life Management*. New York: Warner Books, 1994.

Spencer, Bud. *Altrimenti mi arrabio. La mia vita*. Rome: Alberti Editore, 2010.

Stevens, John. *Budo Secrets: Teachings of the Martial Arts Masters*. Boston: Shambhala Publications, 2002.

Stone, Douglas, Bruce Patton, and Sheila Heen. *Difficult Conversations: How to Discuss What Matters Most*. New York: Penguin Group, 1999.

Sun Tzu. *The Art of War*. Oxford: Oxford University Press, 1983.

Taylor, William C., and Polly La Barre. *Mavericks at Work: Why the Most Original Minds in Business Win*. New York: HarperBusiness, 2006.

"The Hersey-Blanchard Situational Leadership Theory." Mind Tools. http://www.mindtools.com/pages/article/newLDR_44.htm.

"The SOS 'Position.' Boxhall gets all boxed up." All at Sea with Dave Gittins. http://www.titanicebook.com/sospos.html.

Turner, John Rodney, and Stephen J. Simister. *Gower Handbook of Project Management*. Hampshire: Gower Publishing Ltd., 1994.

Vincenzini, Adam. "Thirty Inspiring Quotes about Business, Marketing, and Creativity." *PR Daily* (March 19, 2013). http://www

.prdaily.com/Main/Articles/30_inspiring_quotes_about_
business_marketing_and_c_14073.aspx.

von Oetinger, Bolko, and Henrich von Pierer, eds. *A Passion for Ideas:
How Innovators Create the New and Shape Our World*. West
Lafayette, Indiana: Purdue University Press, 2002.

Womack, James P., and Daniel T. Jones. *Lean Thinking: Banish
Waste and Create Wealth in Your Corporation*. New York:
Productivity Press, 2004.

Weisinger, Hendrie. *The Genius of Instinct: Reclaim Mother Nature's
Tools for Enhancing Your Health, Happiness, Family, and
Work*. Boston: Pearson Education, 2009.

Weinschenk, Susan M. *100 Things Every Designer Needs to Know
About People*. Berkeley: New Riders, 2011.